EARLY SMITHTOWN

by
NORMAN O'BERRY of ST. JAMES
assisted by
EDW. J. HAYDEN
DONAL A. DEVINE
JOHN T. TRENT

THIS MAP HAS BEEN COMPILED AND PRODUCED TO THE BEST OF OUR RECOLLECTION AND ABILITY IN THE YEAR OF THE 200ᵗʰ ANNIVERSARY OF THE INDEPENDENCE OF THE UNITED STATES OF AMERICA.

LEGEND
① 1665-1715 ③ 1765-1815
② 1715-1765 ④ 1815-1865

DATE REFLECTS APPROXIMATE RESIDENCE OF PERSON NAMED.

Smithtown has played an important role in the development of this Island and the Nation

Sincerely
Noel Marsh
3/7/97

The Smithtown Historical Society proudly presents this glimpse of Smithtown's past as seen through the camera lens and the collective memories of its people. We are pleased to bring to our friends and neighbors the pictorial history of Smithtown and its hamlets—Smithtown Branch, St. James, Kings Park, Nesconset, Hauppauge, and Commack.

Author Noel Gish is a distinguished teacher of Long Island History and has had a long association with the Society as a Trustee, volunteer, supporter, and friend. His patient research and tireless efforts to unearth the photographs and stories presented in this book are testimony to his devotion to the story of our past. Noel Gish has produced a highly readable and visually fascinating glimpse of Smithtown. We hope that you too will find it interesting and exciting.

Bank of Smithtown is pleased to have sponsored *Smithtown, New York, 1660–1929: Looking Back Through the Lens* by Noel J. Gish

Proceeds from this beautifully illustrated book will go to benefit the maintenance and preservation of Smithtown's historic properties.

The Smithtown News

The Community's Weekly News Magazine

The Smithtown News from its first issue of March 29, 1945 to the present day, has been guided by a strong sense of community, a conviction that our responsibility is to report objectively and comment fairly on events that effect the Town of Smithtown.

We continue to regularly report on the people, the organizations, the activities which shape our hometown. We seek to understand and call attention to the issues which have to be addressed, the problems which have to be solved, the actions which have to be taken to protect this township's rich history and to prepare for the present and to plan for the future.

Sharing a sense of community remains the focus of The Smithtown News.

Sharing A Sense Of Community

The Smithtown News
*1 Brookside Drive
Smithtown, New York 11787*

... and proud of our history

The Smithtown News was founded in 1945 by Robert James Malone who served as Publisher until his death in 1966. Mr. Malone, prior to starting The News, served as Mayor of Nissequogue Village in 1943 and as Supervisor of the Town of Smithtown 1944-45. Intricately involved with The News since its founding was Virginia Eckels Malone who served as the Town of Smithtown Historian from 1967-78. Mrs. Malone also wrote a weekly column, "News of Long Ago", which was published in The Smithtown News for 30 years.

SMITHTOWN
NEW YORK
1660-1929
LOOKING BACK THROUGH THE LENS

G. B. Brainard was an amateur photographer who took a series of pictures of Smithtown before the arrival of telephones, paved roads and automobiles. This photograph from 1878 captures a muddy Jericho Turnpike, looking west near the "Common Crossing," at the juncture of Jericho Turnpike and Route 25A.

Jericho Turnpike, the "Common Crossing," 1996. The "Common Crossing" as seen in 1996; the recent bridge construction dominates the junction of Route 25 and Route 25A, near the statue of the Bull. This photo is an interesting contrast to the uncluttered scene photographed by Brainard in 1878. Photo by author

Copyright © 1996 by Noel J. Gish and The Smithtown Historical Society

All rights reserved, including the right to reproduce this work in any form whatsoever without permission in writing from the publisher, except for brief passages in connection with a review.

For information write:

The Donning Company/Publishers
184 Business Park Drive, Suite 106
Virginia Beach, Virginia 23462

Steve Mull, General Manager
Debra Y. Quesnel, Project Director
Tracey Emmons-Schneider, Director of Research
Dawn Kofroth, Production Manager
Betsy Bobbitt, Executive Editor
Joseph C. Schnellmann, Graphic Designer
Tony Lillis, Director of Marketing
Teri Arnold, Marketing Assistant

Library of Congress Cataloging-in-Publication Data

Gish, Noel, 1948–
    Smithtown, New York, 1660–1929 : looking back through the lens / by Noel Gish.
        p.   cm.
    Includes bibliographical references and index.
    ISBN 0-89865-980-9 (alk. paper)
    1. Smithtown (N.Y.: Town)—History. 2. Smithtown (N.Y.: Town)—History—Pictorial works. I. Title.
F129.S6127G57   1996
974.7'25—dc20
                                      96-34811
                                                              CIP

Printed in the United States of America

TABLE OF CONTENTS

Acknowledgments 9

Introduction 13

I. In the Beginning 15

II. The Water Brings Life 31

III. The Struggle for Freedom

    and Independence: 1776–1800 45

IV. Life in Smithtown 59

V. The Civil War and Change 83

VI. Hooves, Wheels and Automobiles. 103

VII. Friends and Neighbors:

    The Communities of Smithtown 115

VIII. The New Century: 1900–1929. 167

Bibliography 186

Index. 188

ACKNOWLEDGMENTS

I would like to thank all the many people who have helped in the preparation of this pictorial history of Smithtown. In particular, I would like to express my deep thanks to Louise Hall, director of the Smithtown Historical Society, who gave unselfishly of her time and energy to see the project through; her careful proofreading was invaluable. Brad Harris, President of the Smithtown Historical Society supplied direction, proofread the final manuscript, and supplied a wealth of information through his many devoted years of research as Town Historian and community educator. Robert Mackay, director of the Society for the Preservation of Long Island Antiquities, offered his help and support from the very first. Carol Traynor I thank for her patience and help with the S.P.L.I.A. Collection. Wally Broege, director of the Suffolk County Historical Society, I thank for his help with access to the Hal Fullerton Collection. I also thank David Kerkhof, librarian at Suffolk County Historical Society for his help in locating needed photographs. I must also thank David Allen for his help with the map collection at Stony Brook University Library, Doris Halowitch and the staff at the Long Island Room in the Smithtown Library for the loan of key photographs, Leo Ostebo, director of the Kings Park Heritage Museum, for access to all the materials without any red tape, and the Lake Ronkonkoma Historical Society, especially Marge Raynor, who helped make the whole process much easier.

To the following individuals I owe a great deal of thanks for their help in finding key photographs: Debra Wythe at the Brooklyn Museum; Judy Walsh, director, and Julie Moffet, photographer archivist at the Brooklyn Public Library; the staff at the Queensborough Library, Long Island Collection; Susan Danforth at Brown University Library, Providence, Rhode Island; Mary Engelmann, curator at Northport Historical Society; Brookhaven Town Historian David Overton; Mitzi Caputo, Huntington Historical Society; Natalie Naylor, director of Long Island Studies Institute, Hofstra University; and Barbara Van Liew, historian for Head of the Harbor.

Facing page: 1750 Map of Long Island, "Smith's Town." Map Collection, Library, S.U.N.Y. at Stony Brook

One of the earliest tintype photographs known of Smithtown, circa 1850. Franklin Pierce was President of the United States when Edward Smith's house stood on the south side of Jericho Turnpike, in Head of the River. It was converted, in 1856, to the Riverside Hotel by B. B. Newton.

There were many local people who spent time with me working on photographs, or telling me stories and sharing their experiences. I am truly grateful to : Frank Stepanek, Dick and Marie Sturm, Tim Dempsey, John Valentine, Jane Gambieski, Charles Embree Rockwell, Ralph Meyers, Jack and Elaine Marr, James A. Welsh, postmaster of Smithtown, Robert Saal, Albert Ruoff, Joel Streich, Bradley Rock, president of the Bank of Smithtown, Mr. and Mrs. Edward Walsh, and King Pedlar.

Of course, there were a great many people who responded to the Historical Society's call for photographs. Many thanks to Arthur D. Phillips, Edgar Law Land, Tom Gaynor, John Provenzano, Walter Board, Carole Palmer, Howard Byrne, Tom Stock, Sandy Olsen, Beth Mathews, George McTiernan, Miles Borden, Karen Dongvort, Clara Weisman, Frank Sider, and my colleague, Carl Wampole, who supplied some great pictures of Nesconset, even though he really wanted a book on the Erie Canal.

I received some special photographic help from King Pedlar who worked long and hard in getting some great photographic reproductions and helped refine the work on St. Johnland. A great deal of thanks to Joseph Albert, a great friend, who helped in photography, restoration of some key photos and some special artwork. He came through on every request I made of him. And, finally, to my wonderful family without whom this project would not have been possible. My thanks to my daughter Lindsey Ann who helped with the computer and forgave me for not going on vacation. I owe a great thanks to my son, Noel, who helped type some of the text, got the material untangled from the computer, and also for traveling as my assistant taking pictures of cemeteries during the worst winter snows in decades. A very special thanks to my wife, Elaine, who did just about everything else while I was doing "the book." Elaine did all the typing, proofreading, commenting, advising, retyping, editing, while giving me time, support, help and love in the long months of research and writing.

To all of my family, friends, colleagues, community members, and the trustees and officers of the Historical Society, I express my deep sense of appreciation and gratitude for your help.

G. B. Brainard took this photo labeled "Main Street," Smithtown, 1878. In a little over 120 years the exact location of this photo has been lost. The picket fence indicates Main Street, Jericho Turnpike, Middle Country Road, but where? Can you help?

INTRODUCTION

There have been tremendous changes in Smithtown since the days when the first Americans hunted the woodlands and fished the rich ponds and streams. Changes were wrought by Richard Smith and his family. Farms replaced woodlands, European varieties of apples and pears replaced the native stands of chestnut and cedar. Many of these changes were beneficial to the people looking for an escape from poverty, oppression, and discrimination. Often change brings regret as the land and its innocence are replaced by monuments to man. Often these monuments are built out of necessity, sometimes out of ignorance. Many beautiful places we remembered from our youth are gone, as are the places our forefathers remembered. Even as we Americans push into the twenty-first century with hope, there is regret in what has passed and what innocence has been forever lost.

The beauty of the land, the people, and the places of interest must somehow be preserved. If these things cannot be preserved in a physical sense, then they must be preserved in our historical records. Those who follow must be aware that there were many who came before to help smooth the way. The houses, roads, businesses, and playgrounds are the traces of passing generations. A family photo, a letter, a marriage certificate, and even a tax bill are relics of a bygone era.

This book is an attempt to depict some of the interesting facets of our community. It is hoped that the words and pictures will trigger a memory or two and may cause a young man or woman to engage in a conversation with a parent, grandparent, or neighbor to ask about "the good old days." Hopefully, pictures will emerge from attics, closets, and cellars to see the light of day once more. For only in the memories of those who lived can the past really be examined and understood.

No claim is made to the completeness of this work. There are many stories and pictures that were not included. More work will be necessary to bring this up to the present. The text and pictures are necessarily brief, limited by time and space. It is hoped that this book will only whet the reader's appetite to pursue an even deeper study of our town and its people.

A wigwam was constructed by the Long Island Archeological Association at Hoyt Farm, New Highway, Commack. An animal skin would have covered the entrance, while smoke from the interior fires was vented through a hole in the top. Suffolk Archeological Association Project, Hoyt Farm

CHAPTER 1

In the Beginning

SMITHTOWN: WHO ARE WE?

Smithtown is an area that is roughly fifty-five square miles and lies midway along the north shore of the largest island adjoining the continental United States. Only fifty miles from the great metropolis of New York City, Smithtown shares aspects of both an urban and rural community. The sound of a busy bustling intersection is only a short distance from the quiet of a canoe winding its way down the Nissequogue River. The area is so varied and so diverse that no single picture can adequately capture its true identity.

The people of Smithtown are as varied as the landscape. There is no "typical" Smithtown resident. From a community that began with one English family along the Nissequogue River, the composition of the town's people has continuously undergone change. In the 1690s Smithtown already had people from France and Holland, along with African Americans, who were brought here as slaves. In the town census of 1776, the total population had reached only 716 persons, and a good portion of them were descendants of the Yorkshire Englishman Richard Smith. Over the following decades new groups of immigrants, seeking opportunity, found their way to Smithtown. In the census of 1880, the population had risen to 2,249, almost triple what it had been only one hundred years earlier. Irish Catholics and Russian Jews escaping famine and persecution came to work as laborers at the Kings County Hospital, or to open shops and businesses. They came to Smithtown seeking economic opportunity and on the way built homes and churches and raised their families.

The community of Smithtown was growing. By 1950 the numbers showed a town population of 20,993, and many people saw the beginnings of a suburban community. Rural Smithtown was fast becoming a distant memory.

The next twenty years, however, proved to be the most dramatic for the town and its people. By 1970 the population boomed to 114,000, a 50 percent increase in only twenty years. Although the growth has slowed since 1970, Smithtown is still coping with the stressful affects brought on by the rapid development after World War II. The need for housing, schools, hospitals, and town support services has created enormous problems that continue to be addressed.

The 1990 census showed some stabilization in the population which gives the present-day Smithtown a breathing spell. There may be time for more careful planning and long range proposals to address future concerns. This rest period of development has also generated a concern by citizens for the preservation of those natural and historic treasures that are worthy of our attention.

As Smithtown and the nation race into the next century and a new millennium, we should take some time to pause and reflect on the time that has passed us by.

NATIVE AMERICANS

Smithtown was inhabited long before Richard Smith and his family. Native Americans, speaking the Algonquin language, walked the land centuries before European sails were sighted off Long Island's shores. The Nesequakes were a small band, probably numbering no more than five hundred members. A primitive people, the Nesequake band lived with ten to fifteen other Native American groups on an island they called Paumanauk. Using stone tools, they hunted, fished, and farmed the land for over 4000 years. In almost total harmony with the earth, they gathered clams and oysters from the mud flats along the river and the bay. All kinds of nuts, berries, onions, and grapes were collected from the fields and woodlands. Animals such as deer, rabbits, squirrels and raccoons were part of their diet. Fish of all types, including fresh and saltwater species were harvested from the local waters. The local Indians did not have horses, pigs, goats, sheep, chickens, or cattle until they were imported to Long Island by the Europeans.

The land was not farmed in the traditional European manner. Small patches of corn, beans, and squash were planted to supplement an island already rich in food resources. Tobacco was also grown and smoked at gatherings or ceremonial events. Constructed of wood bark or thatch, small dome-shaped shelters called wigwams dotted the landscape. Evidence of long house construction, typical of upstate Indian dwellings, was discovered in Smithtown in the 1990s.

A thorough study of these first Americans has been difficult. The Nesequake Indians had no written alphabet and, therefore, no formal written history. There was a cultural discrimination that existed from the very first moment of contact with the European explorers and settlers. The native islanders were considered inferior and not worthy of extensive historical

The grinding stone and platform was found near Lake Ronkonkoma. It is similar to a mortar and pestle and was used for grinding corn and nuts. Lake Ronkonkoma Historical Society

left: This full-grooved ax was found during restoration of the Judge Lawrence Smith Homestead at 205 Middle Country Road. The Native American artifact was unearthed from below the parlor floor in the 1980s. Smithtown Historical Society

right: The name of the route traveling north through Kings Park is known as Indian Head Road. The Nesaquake people claimed that the stone head, placed atop a large rock near Fresh Pond, watched and protected the native people as they walked the nearby path. Legend said that if the stone head were ever removed it would somehow find its way to the rock and resume its vigil. David Smith recorded that the stone carving could still be seen into the late 1790s. By that time, the Indians of Smithtown were all but gone and shortly after the stone head vanished as well. Indian Head Road has changed over the years. It was straightened, widened, and covered with macadam leaving only its name unchanged. However, some years ago, an odd looking stone was conveyed to the Smithtown Historical Society. One can only wonder if the stone carving of Indian Head Road has, indeed, returned once again. Smithtown Historical Society

analysis. Although there is some written history, much of it was written by the early settlers or ministers who misunderstood or misinterpreted the culture of these first islanders. Much of what is recorded comes in the form of land transactions or deeds made between Europeans and native peoples.

The first recorded deed in Smithtown was made in 1650, and not by Richard Smith. A group of land speculators from Connecticut, including brothers Edmund, Jonas, Jeremy, and Timothy Wood, along with Daniel Whitehead and Stephen Hudson, signed an agreement with Nasseconseke (Nesconset), the Sachem (leader) of the Nesequake Indians. The Indians agreed to convey an amount of land for trade goods that included: "Six coats, six fathoms of wampum, six hoes, six hatchets, six knives, six kettles, one hundred muxes [muskets] to be paid on or before the 29th of

Artifacts like these are common at archeological digs in Smithtown and throughout Long Island. Top left—a broken piece of pottery (sherd), with simple line decorations; and top right—a small stone vessel, or Indian paint pot. Below are projectile points including arrowheads, made mostly of quartz stone. These points could be fashioned to an almost razor sharp edge. The large blade on the left was probably mounted in a handle and used as a knife. Collection of the author

September, 1650." The land deal, although finalized with the Nesequake band, was never recorded with the English or Dutch governments as required. This failure to gain registration left the door open for Richard Smith's claim years later.

Little is left of the Nesequake people and their history. Although the Nesequake Indians were well suited for working the land, they were no match for the more advanced European culture. The gunpowder, metal tools, intoxicating beverages, and new diseases were overpowering for people living a simpler way. Disease was probably the single most significant factor in the Nesequake decline. A plague of 1658–59, along with a small pox epidemic of 1662, reduced the entire native population by two-thirds. By 1776 the influence of Native Americans on Smithtown development was over. There are no significant historical remarks about the Nesequake people after that point in our town's history.

The most serious historical examination of our first town residents is being carried out through archeological studies. The study of artifacts left behind gives historians the best insight into who these people were and how they lived. The rapid development of Long Island and Smithtown since 1950 has probably destroyed many significant sites. The less densely populated areas of Nissequogue and Head of the Harbor may still hold vast archeological evidence that will enable future generations to probe deeper into Smithtown's Indian heritage.

There are traces of the past hidden in the very words we speak today. If you speak these words slowly, carefully and without our "Lang Eyeland" accent, you might hear echoes of the island's first people. Commac, Hauppauge, Nissequogue, Rassapeague, Ronkonkoma, Moriches, and Sherrewogue are just some of the place names left behind by the Algonquin Indians who centuries ago lived upon this land.

RICHARD SMITH

No formal examination of the history of Smithtown can begin without some attention being paid to its founder, Richard Smythe. Much like any story of settlement in America in the seventeenth century, the beginnings are found in the old world. The population of England was mushrooming from three million people in 1550 to more than four million by the time of Richard Smythe's birth in 1613. This booming population, of which Richard Smythe was a part, was spreading out over England's evergreen countryside. Even the area of Yorkshire in northern England, the place of Richard's birth, was feeling pressure. The great lords of England had begun an enclosure movement. Large areas were fenced off for private sheep raising, forcing even established sheep ranchers of Yorkshire off the land.

When economic depression struck in the 1590s combined with the enclosure movements, thousands of yeoman took to the roads. This mobile population alarmed the more noble of the English countryside. The conclusion was that England was burdened with a surplus population. Economic change coupled with religious unrest created a climate of uncertainty. The King of England, Charles I, aimed at purging troublesome malcontents from the English Church. Puritans were definitely not popular. Although Charles severed no heads among the Puritans, he removed some ears and this whole situation of official Anglicanization was unsettling. It was unsettling to Irish Catholics and Presbyterians of Scotland and the independent-minded folk of Yorkshire. Freedom of religion, or religious thought, was a great concern for many who themselves had not yet been the subject of persecution.

What was the cause of Richard's departure? Was it economic insecurity, the cruel religious repression of Charles I, or fear of continued unrest and civil war? Maybe it was just a strong desire to own a large land holding that America could now offer and England could not. Whatever the cause, Richard Smythe sailed from England in October of 1635. At age twenty-two, Richard was aboard the ship *John of London*, bound for St. Christophers in the West Indies in the New World. Richard's voyage may have ended when his ship made land in New England or he may have continued on to the West Indies and St. Kitts. His exact movements are not known, but he was in Massachusetts Bay Colony by 1637. Possibly he chose to settle at Rowley, Massachusetts, where in 1630 a settlement had been made by families hailing from his native Yorkshire. Records indicate that Richard had some contact in nearby Boston and Cambridge by 1640. It will not be until his arrival on Long Island and the town of Southampton that a more definitive record of Richard emerges. What caused Smythe to leave Massachusetts is not clear. What history can tell us is that by 1640 Massachusetts Bay had become a closed society. Only Puritans could vote and be elected to office. Leadership roles would be granted, not on merit, but on membership. Roger Williams had already fled the Bay Colony and established his own land holding of Rhode Island. Anne Hutchinson, the great dissenter, was banished to New York in 1638. It is quite possible that Richard Smythe could not be made to conform and, like Williams, Hutchinson and others, he would leave.

Families from the town of Lynn in Massachusetts Bay Colony had journeyed across Long Island Sound to Southampton in June 1640. Richard Smythe was not among the original settlers, but it seems he was driven to Long Island by the same forces. Richard does not appear in the town records until 1643, so he probably arrived sometime after 1640. Within a short time, however, Richard was making a name for himself. Records from Southampton indicate that in March 1647 the General Court chose five men, including Richard Smythe, with the power "to give or let land." On October 7, 1648, Richard was named a "freeman and head of his family." This indicates a marriage by that time, more than likely to Sarah. A year later in 1649, Richard Smythe and Richard Odell were appointed by Southampton to "lay out part of the 'great plains' to be fenced."

In March of 1654 Richard reached a high rank of social and economic importance. He was named to lead one of the four wards that would patrol the beach to cut up and tie down drift whales. Onshore whaling, or the use of beached whales, was a source of considerable wealth to early Long Island settlements. Whale oil was used to fuel lamps. The whale bone could be used to make buttons, clothespins, and a myriad of other items. Being named to head a ward was a great honor and records indicate that men of the fourth ward were referred to as "Mr. Smythe's squadron."

By 1654 Richard had become one of only a half dozen in the town who were depended upon to lead in public service. Very few names appear more frequently in Southampton records than that of Richard Smythe. On or about September 17, 1656, an incident occurred which would forever change the history of the Smythe family. "It is ordered by the general court that Richard Smythe for his Irreverent carriage towards the magistrates contrary to the order was adjudged to be banished out of the towne and he is to have a weeks liberty to prepare himself to depart, and if at any time he be found after this limited week within the town or the bounds thereof he shall forfeit twenty shillings." Southampton records do not reveal the reason for banishment. Richard's fierce Yorkshire independence or his strong personal or religious convictions may have played a part in his "irreverent" actions. Perhaps Richard may have found himself in a power struggle with other magistrates in the town. Whatever the cause of banishment, the events destined Richard for even greater heights of political power and prestige.

A turn-of-the-century photograph of Edmund Thomas Smith's property is traditionally considered the site of the original Smith Homestead in the 1660s. Mrs. Amanda Hawks, Smithtown Historical Society

After selling his house and lots, Richard migrated to Setauket in Brookhaven and became a resident by 1657. It seemed his banishment from Southampton left little ill feeling among the residents of his new home town. However, in 1660 Richard did find himself engaged in court in a civil dispute with Mr. John Young, a Setauket resident. This incident was to be another in a long line of legal cases that would involve Richard Smythe. There were very few times in his life that he was not engaged in some civil suit in a court of justice in the state or county.

It is not known when the idea of acquiring the neighboring Nissequogue lands first occurred to Richard. He had been in Setauket for almost four years by 1661 and had ample opportunity to become acquainted with the area which had not been appropriated by formal deed or patent. We do know that Richard witnessed the signing of a deed by which Sachem Wyandanch gave Nissequogue land to Lion Gardiner in 1659. The deed was a gift given in gratitude for Gardiner's assistance in securing the safe return of the Sachem's daughter who had been kidnapped. In 1663 Lion Gardiner conveyed the title to Richard Smythe for reasons not recorded. Conflicting stories say that the land was sold, given or gambled away in a card game. Curiously, Wyandanch died the year that he conveyed the lands to Gardiner and Gardiner died the year that he transferred title to Smythe. If there was any written agreement in the latter transaction, it has never been found. However, David, son of Lion, endorsed the original deed to Smith, October 15, 1664, indicating that he knew of the arrangment and was bound by it. The deed now in Richard's hands secured for him the Nissequogue property.

From the English point of view, land and legal title were conveyed to individuals in the form of grants or patents. The deed from Gardiner was the first step. Smythe was then expected to satisfy Indian occupants and secure additional deeds confirming descriptions to his property boundaries.

Conflicting claims to his property kept Richard Smythe legally occupied for nearly twelve more years until he was officially undisputed patentee of the area. Smythe was aware that an earlier deed to the Nesequake lands existed. In 1650 Nassetconset (Nesconset), the Sachem of the Nessequake, had given a deed to Edmund Wood and others for land along the Nissequogue. In a deed dated 1663 Richard indicated that he had secured the title from the original grantees. These earlier "settlers" had been only land speculators and had not made settlement or formally registered their claim in either English or Dutch courts. Richard Smythe moved quickly and in June 1664 attempted to confirm his authority by taking his petition to the English government in General Court in Hartford, Connecticut. Hartford was the capital since Suffolk had been designated as part of Connecticut in 1650. Richard's timing was off by just a bit. In 1664, as he was making his claim in Hartford, Charles II, King of England, redistributed land rights in the New World. The Duke of York, the King's brother, was given control over the New England area including Long Island. The island was then placed under governmental control of New York. Sir Richard Nicolls was the governor whom Mr. Smythe would have to petition to secure his claim.

Richard Smythe was persistent and he secured his first patent on March 3, 1665. It covered all the land east of the Nissequogue "and on the west side of the river so far as is at present in ye possession of Richard Smythe."

The failure of the Nicolls Patent to secure title to the west side of the Smithtown tract dragged on for years. Huntington claimed that a Matinecock deed granting them the land predated the deed to Wyandance. Smith claimed that the Matinecocks sold land that did not rightfully belong to them so the Huntington deed was void. The matter of Smythe's western claim was in the English court in 1673 when the Dutch recaptured New York and Long Island in the Anglo-Dutch wars. Again, without batting an eye, Smythe changed his legal direction and headed into the Dutch court, where the court verbally ruled in his favor. However, before the ruling could be printed and recorded, the war ended and the Dutch ceded New York back to the English in the Treaty of November 10, 1674. Richard "bulled" his way forward and pressed his suit before the new English administration to obtain a final judgment on October 13, 1675. A new patent from Governor

Edmund Andros, dated March 25, 1677, conveyed the disputed Nesaquake lands to Smythe and not Huntington.

Somewhere in the middle of this entire patent designation comes the famous "Bull Story." Whether fact or fiction, it is a wonderful mixture that rivals the stories of Pocahontas and John Smith or even Captain Miles Standish at Plymouth Bay. There is no other town on Long Island that can boast of such a delightful story and commemorate it with a five-ton bronze bull. The image of the bull is part of the Richard Smythe story. Richard's coat of arms does depict a bull above a shield with six fleur de lis. It was the "persistence of a bull" that allowed Smith to reaffirm authority over his land time and time again. Maybe Smith had issued a concordat with the various governmental powers. During the sixteenth century "papal bulls," or concordats, were issued to conclude preexisting friction or hostilities between church and state. It is possible that Smith issued his own personal "Smith Bull" to resolve the friction between himself, the Nessequakes, the Dutch, the English, or even the towns of Huntington or Brookhaven. Richard Smythe was a learned man and seemed to know the law very well. He had left England knowing the power of the Papal Bull "Exsurge Domine" which had been issued in 1520. He knew that Papal Bulls could settle boundary disputes between dioceses or parishes and establish property or possession rights. Richard, in "getting on his bull," may have done nothing more than make a strong statement of the facts in the case. Mr. Smythe may only have been taking his case to court. The stubborn, energetic leader was not going to be beaten by the legal system as he had been in Southampton years earlier. He would not be banished from his land again. Richard would "bull" his way, if necessary, to win a complete patent to the land he felt was legally his by deed and settlement.

Smythe did establish his control over the Nesequake territory in an English region of Long Island known as East Riding. Riding was a name taken from England. It was one of three divisions in Yorkshire—North, East and West Riding. In reality Richard Smythe may have been issuing political control, the "bull," over his territory in "East Riding." The facts should not get in the way of a good tale. Richard and his bull make a much better story than any logical development of historical evidence one might present. It is like Santa Claus or Johnny Appleseed or the stories of Daniel Boone, Davey Crockett or even George Washington. There will always be flying reindeer and chopped cherry trees in our myths and legends. No one should dispute a good story.

Artifacts from seventeenth-century America are rare. Those items documented from the family of Richard Smythe are rarer still. This chair, owned by the 'Bull Rider', has been cared for through the centuries by Smith family members.

This stoneware pitcher, of English origin, dates from the early 1600s and was a proud possession of the early Smythe family. Smithtown Historical Society Collection

Having secured his deed from Lion Gardiner, Richard Smythe still had to make a deal with the local natives. Nesconset, Sachem of the Nesequake band of Indians living along the river, agreed that Smythe could have all the land he could circumnavigate from sunrise to sunset while riding on the back of his bull. Waiting until the longest day of the year, June 21st (Smythe was a smart man), Richard took his bull "Whisper" and rode around the boundaries of present-day Smithtown. Carefully, he blazed trees along the way to show the Nesequake band the vast dimension of his holdings. Resting at noon in a hollow between Huntington and Smithtown, he noshed on bread and cheese. (Ah! Bread and Cheese Hollow Road, I get it!). Then, Richard continued his quest to complete the circuit of the township by nightfall. The effort which Smythe would have made was extraordinary. Even the author's father's epic stories of following General Patton through Europe in 1944–45 pale in comparison. Smythe rode close to fifty miles through heavily wooded, previously untraveled wilderness on an animal known for endurance, but not speed. Supporters of the feat tell of an extraordinary man, who with fierce determination and planning, had carefully trained his bull for this Olympian event. Still others say that the night before his famous ride, Richard took a cow out of the barn, one of Whisper's favorites, and under cover of darkness, walked the cow around the same area, leaving a telling female scent. The next morning, Whisper picked up the scent and took off in pursuit of his lady love at a phenomenal pace. The problem with the last story is that we now have Richard Smythe traveling close to a hundred miles in twenty-four hours, traveling fifty miles with a cow in the dark, then getting up bright and early to travel the same with the famous bull Whisper. No wonder he stopped for bread and cheese at noon. It seems that the name of the cow was never recorded, nor does she share any part of the recognition for an immortal feat of endurance.

Whatever the marriage of fact and fiction, some points must be made clear. Richard Smythe would have made a mark on Long Island history with or without Whisper. He had been a bold man even to venture to the new world. As a settler on Long Island, he had become a leader through his intelligence, temperament, and strength of character. Richard was called "Mister" even in the earliest of records, a title which historian Elias Pelletreau calls "not then an unmeaning compliment." Richard, having secured his claim, got on with governing his domain for the remainder of his life. His wife, Sarah, bore him nine children: Jonathan, Obadiah, Richard, Job, Daniel, Adam, Samuel, Elizabeth and Deborah. Sarah is an interesting and often forgotten member of the Smythe Family. Richard's marriage to Sarah has been the subject of much debate. Tradition held that Sarah's maiden name was Folger. Some new genealogical evidence supports the possibility that Richard's wife was not Sarah Folger, but Sarah Hammond of Watertown, Massachusetts. The marriage between Richard and Sarah took

Obadiah Smith's grave is clearly visible in this 1895 photo by Mrs. Amanda Hawks. Obadiah, son of Richard, died tragically in a drowning accident in the Nissequogue River in 1680. Somewhere near Obadiah is the grave of Richard Smythe, patentee; the exact grave site is unknown. Mrs. Amanda Hawks, Smithtown Historical Society

place sometime around 1640 and before his departure for Southampton.

Sarah, whatever her original maiden name, was a strong partner for Richard. Both names are found prominently on deeds and transfers of the period. Upon Richard's death on March 7, 1692, the Smith lands were divided almost equally among all of his children, except his daughter Elizabeth. She had married and moved to New Jersey by 1680; her considerable influence led to the creation of a town that bears her name—Elizabeth, New Jersey.

Richard and his wife did not follow the old lines of primogeniture, but divided the land without regard to age or sex. The 1692 will was signed by both Richard and Sarah. She claimed a joint interest in the property and the right to dispose of it. Sarah continued to reside in the family home until her death almost sixteen years later in 1708. Her will, upon her death, shows a desire to be fair and equitable with all of her children. She attempted to "prevent future difference among my children" by nullifying all debts owed her or her husband. The 1692 date is also significant in the evolution of the Smythe Family name. At this point, the spelling of the family name changes to SMITH, and remains so even today. The first chapter to Smithtown's founding family had been written as the town journeyed into the beginning of the eighteenth century.

Question: What two famous sculptures were originally made in France, sit high atop a pedestal and can be found in the United States today? Answer: The statue of the Smithtown Bull and the Statue of Liberty; both are famous landmarks in New York, but only one graces the intersection of Jericho Turnpike and St. Johnland Road (Route 25A). A. Biren Postcard, Smithtown Historical Society

In 1929 the Rumsey statue of the Bull sat, not in Smithtown, but outside the entrance to the Brooklyn Museum. The Bull was part of a major exhibit on display between 1929 and 1932. Afterward the bronze casting was placed in storage. Amazingly, the bull's nickname "Whisper" does not appear in any early Smythe family records. Magically, the name began to appear around 1900, as the legend of Richard Smythe and his famous bovine grew to immense proportions. Brooklyn Museum Collection

THE BULL

The statue of "Whisper," the Smithtown bull, merits a story of its very own. In 1903 Mr. Lawrence Smith Butler, a descendent of the town founder, proposed the idea of a bronze statue to his friend and classmate, American sculptor Charles Cary Rumsey. Butler believed that money could be raised to pay for the project, so models were made and a price of $12,000 was agreed upon for the completed work. In 1923 the "bigger than life" casting was complete and ready for shipment. However, in Smithtown the funds had not been raised and Lawrence Butler became frustrated.

Rumsey patiently waited for over five years with no success. In 1932 Charles Rumsey died and the added burden of the depression seemed to doom the project. In 1941 Butler renewed his quest. He convinced the Town Board to build a concrete pedestal to hold the statue, raised the $1750 needed to cover the cost of the move, and convinced Rumsey's heirs to donate the statue to the town. First by truck, then via railroad, and then by truck once more, the fourteen-foot, five-ton bronze bull made its long awaited journey. On May 10, 1941, Mary Rumsey, daughter of the sculptor and wife of New York Governor W. Averill Harriman, presented the statue to the people of Smithtown. After almost forty years of effort, Lawrence Smith Butler had triumphed in his efforts to immortalize the famous Bull of Richard Smith.

In 1878 photographer G. B. Brainard burned an image onto the glass plate of his camera. This remarkable image, looking west, shows the juncture of Jericho Turnpike and St. Johnland Road (Route 25A). The Arthur Store is on the right, the train trestle is on the left. The flag pole in the center of the photo shows where the statue of the Smithtown Bull can be found today. G. B. Brainard, Society for the Preservation of Long Island Antiquities

GRAVESTONES

Historians have used gravestones designs, inscriptions, and even stone placement to gain insight into early Long Island culture. The names of early Smithtown settlers, their births, deaths, and even family relationships can be established through a study of grave sites. Tombstones, markings, or "graven images" provide a fascinating body of evidence for genealogists and historians. At first, early settlers marked graves with wooden posts or headboards. By the 1670s carved headstones filled with symbolic images began to appear and they became a regular feature of graveyard markings after that time. How the carved symbols on gravestones changed tells much about how people's attitudes and values were shifting with the passage of time. The old burying ground of the Nissequogue, the Presbyterian Church, the Hauppauge Methodist, Wheeler and others in the town can provide information that would otherwise be lost.

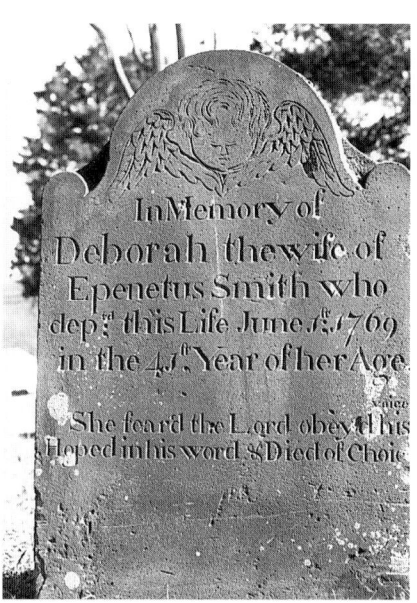

Equal rights for women were yet to be established. In 1769 Deborah is known only as the wife of Epenetus Smith. Without marriage records Deborah's maiden name is lost to historians and genealogists. Her brief epitaph sheds some light on the possible reason for her death at the young age of forty-one years. Smithtown Presbyterian Cemetery

This grim skull carving on the gravestone of Mary Arthur represents the vivid intensity with which early Smithtown residents faced death. The death's head motif was used widely in the seventeenth and into the mid-eighteenth century to convey the puritanical concern that life is transitory and that salvation is not automatically granted to those who merely believed. Emphasis on life as a preparation for the afterlife is reinforced in these early gravestone mottoes. Smithtown Presbyterian Cemetery

By the second quarter of the eighteenth century, attitudes toward death and religion were changing as gravestone iconography attests. The ever-present death's heads are replaced by smiling cherubs or winged angels. The winged image of Ruth Brewster, who died in April 1793, represents the flight of the soul heavenward. This romantic design tells us much about the secularization of Smithtown and the passing of early Puritan intense seriousness about the redemption of mankind. Less morbid introspection and more hopefulness was spreading through Puritan thought. The carvings reveal changing life experiences and values. Smith Family Cemetery, Nissequogue

Carvings were added like hands pointing skyward, pictures of lambs, flowers, or in this case, a sentimentalized willow tree. The carvings, by the mid-nineteenth century, became less threatening and more reassuring. The headstones of Connecticut sandstone were replaced by other more durable stones like schist or marble. Hauppauge Methodist Cemetery

The simple headstone of Paul Smith illustrates a problem with gravestone preservation—weathering. The constant stress of temperature changes, precipitation, the modern addition of air pollution and acid rain, coupled with reckless acts of vandalism have accelerated the loss of these earliest gravestones. Paul Smith's marker will continue to weather and erode. Within the next fifty years, few of these early headstones will be found intact amid the cemeteries in town. Smithtown Presbyterian Cemetery

This 1927 aerial view shows the Nissequogue River at Landing Avenue Bridge looking north. The area, commonly known as Blydenburgh's Landing in the eighteenth century, had been deeded by Richard Smythe for town use. In 1806 a dock was constructed by the town for the convenience of its residents. P. Hildebrand, photographer, Smithtown Historical Society

CHAPTER 2

The Water Brings Life

THE NISSEQUOGUE RIVER

It is the river, the Nissequogue, that brought life to the land. The water that flows along its banks was the source of power and wealth that helped create early settlement. Richard Smith knew its importance, and so, too, did the Native Americans who roamed the river system that still bears their Algonquin name. The Nissequogue was created as the last glaciers retreated from Long Island about twenty thousand years ago. The watershed region of the river is only twenty-seven square miles, but it exists almost entirely in the township of Smithtown. Far more than just a fresh water estuary, the Nissequogue is a complex living system that has helped nourish a community of living plants and animals. Tulip trees grew which Native Americans shaped into dugout canoes. The river supports a vast array of wildlife. Snowy egrets, hawks, ospreys, and various song birds inhabit the river from one end to the other. Foxes, raccoons, and rat-tailed opossum scout a region once inhabited by an abundant deer population as well.

The river has worked nature's magic for thousands of years, first for the Indians and then for the Colonial settlers. Using weirs made of tree branches, set along muddy flats, the Indians trapped fish during the change of tides. All kinds of marine life called the river home. Brook trout, striped bass, weak fish, bluefish, flounders, eel, shad, and sturgeon all thrived here and helped supply a food source to Smithtown residents. The life blood of the town flowed through this artery for over 250 years sustaining its people. The river creatures gave the river a pulse, and with every rise and fall of the tide new life would flow. Besides being a nursery and spawning ground for fish, shellfish like oysters, clams, and mussels grew along the mud flats near the mouth of the river, and crustaceans like the blue claw crab scavenged the river bottom and provided tasty meals. The shellfish grew to enormous size and in great numbers, again helping to supply people with a renewable food resource.

Richard Smith understood the value, power, and majesty of this island river. It was the river that helped sustain him and his family. Early townspeople could set a table with a wide variety of salt and freshwater fish.

A view from the Kings Park bluff looks eastward across the mouth of the Nissequogue River. A sloop rests at the "Old Dock" at Kings Park. Short Beach, acquired by the town in 1907, lies almost empty except for a lone beach house near the point, circa 1900. Smithtown Historical Society Collection

In 1856 Benjamin Newton converted the home of Edward Smith (great grandson of Richard) into the Riverside Hotel. In 1901 the hotel was remodeled by William Spurge, who operated the hotel until Frank Friede became the owner and operator in 1918. Smithtown Historical Society

An unending supply of oysters, clams and blue claw crabs were there for the taking. The Nissequogue turned the first mill constructed in the region. The first commercial center was established at the "Head of the River."

The river harbored a shipbuilding industry almost unknown to twentieth-century Smithtown residents. An oyster sloop, *Nellie A. Ryle,* was built by Slope and Scudder in 1818. It measured thirty-five feet, a width of over twelve feet, and drew under four feet of water. Crafted for river and Sound operation, it can still be found today as a valuable exhibit at the Marine Museum in Mystic, Connecticut.

Other ships were constructed. The 129-foot brig *Tanner* was built in 1855, probably launched along the river at a point called *Ships Hole*. The ship remained active until the First World War. Captain Frank Hawkins, who lived on the east bank of the river, was known to have built a number of vessels. The last was constructed in 1891, an eight-ton sloop named the *Nellie*, which sailed out of Port Jefferson for many years.

The coming of the railroad in 1872, and the telegraph in November 1880, made rural Smithtown accessible to the big city to the west. The writings of Henry David Thoreau spoke to America about simple existence with nature. In the 1880s there were the beginnings of a "back to nature" movement, as America moved closer to an urban environment. The woods, fields, and streams that encompass the Nissequogue system became an

accessible paradise. The river could provide the city dweller with a weekend shoot or early morning fishing expedition.

The Brooklyn Gun Club was organized to lay claim to the wilderness of the upper river. By 1882 the club changed its name to The Wyandanch Club, to honor the Montauk Sachem so famous in Smithtown history. The club controlled one of the most productive brook trout streams in New York State. Thousands upon thousands of fingerling trout were released into the river by club managers. Nothing could compare to the delicate pink meat of a freshly caught brook trout. Only minutes before, it had been pulled from the cold waters of the Nissequogue, and now was served in noble fashion by the staff at the Wyandanch Club.

In the 1880s brown trout and rainbow trout, both European imports, were stocked in the river to add more to the Old World fly casting tradition. The *Brooklyn Eagle* reported on January 21, 1927, that the Wyandanch Gun Club "released 4000 pheasant for the members to follow." The ring-necked pheasant was not a native bird, but an Asian import brought to Smithtown for the hunting enthusiast. The abundance of game, either domestic or imported, was making Smithtown a hunter's or fisherman's paradise.

Scows transported freight upstream from the docks at the mouth of the river. Supplies of cordwood await shipment downriver. Docks had been constructed by Aaron Smith and Elias Smith, along with Hamilton and Benjamin Darling. All of these people hoped to profit from the river commerce. The first wooden bridge crossing the river east to west was built in 1805 in the area called "the common crossing." G. B. Brainard, 1878, Society for the Preservation of Long Island Antiquities

The Head of the River was alive with development in 1878. Numerous buildings surround Newtons Hotel. E. L. Arthur's Riverside Store is across the road on the left and a lumberyard is located across the river between the hotel and barn. None of these structures remain today. G. B. Brainard, 1878, Society for the Preservation of Long Island Antiquities

Riverside Inn looking east from the trestle, circa 1912. The old wooden bridge has been replaced by an iron bridge. R. S. Feather, Smithtown Historical Society

The Ketcham Brothers operated a dredging company that maintained a river depth suitable for the scows working the river, circa 1910. R. S. Feather, collection of Richard and Marie Sturm

Schooners or sloops that did not clear the river at flood tide had to be secured along the bank. There was a deep pocket in the river that measured sixteen feet even at low tide. This pool was simply known as "Ships hole," and was probably the site of early shipbuilding activity. Faith Smith, Smithtown Historical Society

The Landing Avenue bridge was first constructed in 1806 and rebuilt in 1869. An iron bridge replaced wood in 1902 and was built by the Groton Bridge Company. The Thompson House, as seen around 1910, still stands. R. S. Feather, collection of the author

The fall timetable for the Long Island Railroad from 1887 showed a Brooklyn Bridge stretching from New York City to Long Island. Pictures of fishing and hunting equipment along with scallop shells and pictures of Montauk enticed the city dweller to come east. Smithtown Historical Society

Landing Avenue—this could be entitled "Congestion, 1919." R. S. Feather, collection of Carl Wampole

Mills Family of the Landing out for a "formal" boating, circa 1910. Smithtown Historical Society

Daniel Webster (1782–1852), the great Senator from Massachusetts, was a frequent guest at the Aaron Vail farm. The Nissequogue supplied Mr. Webster and his friends with some of the best trout fishing in the northeast in the 1830s. The Vail house can still be seen on the south side of Jericho Turnpike in the Caleb Smith State Park. R. S. Feather, Smithtown Historical Society

The town's earliest records indicate that the river supplied a vast amount of oysters and clams. Vessels carried bushels of shellfish to New York and Connecticut. The Nissequogue Canning Company operated on Oakside Drive through the 1920s, until river pollution and dredging severely limited production. R. S. Feather, 1913, collection of Carl Wampole

The Brooklyn Gun Club acquired the land around Webster Pond and Willow Pond in 1870. Located on the north side of Jericho Turnpike, near the Caleb Smith I House, Willow Pond was the site of some early fishing lessons. Hal Fullerton Collection, Suffolk County Historical Society

Efforts were made to enhance recreational fishing. The Rassapeaque Club was located north of Landing Avenue Bridge on the east side of the river. It was an exclusive men's fishing and hunting facility located along River Road. R. S. Feather, 1908, Smithtown Historical Society

The Nissequogue Trout Club built large earthenwork ponds to hold trout before releasing them into the river. The club included men, women, and children but refused membership to Smithtown residents. All fish had to be caught on artificial flies, similar to the rules at Caleb Smith Park today. Hal Fullerton Collection, Suffolk County Historical Society

Mr. Charles M. Higgins, a Brooklyn resident but summer visitor, had cement ponds constructed on his property around 1912. These ponds, like others at the Rassapeaque Club, were for holding trout. Bernard Olivie was in charge of construction on the east side of the river. Collection of Tom Stock

Hunting as well as fishing was practiced by the clubs along the river. There was an abundance of ducks and geese. Carvers like Boris Radoyevich, Elias Seaman, and others in the Smithtown area carefully made decoys to lure the real birds into shooting range. Carvers of the 1870s to the 1920s were renowned for their artistry and skill. Collection of the author

The 1900s brought more summer people to Smithtown and the river. The Kenyon family built an estate on the western shore on Oakside Drive. Recreational activities like canoeing and boating became more common as commercial river use waned in the twentieth century. Collection of Tom Stock

Mill Interior, collection of the author

This photo taken in the early 1900s shows two mills. The mill on the left was the gristmill and on right was the sawmill. The great millpond in the back of the photo is now part of the Caleb Smith Park. Only the gristmill remains of this milling complex, having been converted into a home by the White family in the 1930s. R. S. Feather, 1907, collection of the author

This view shows the whole mill complex at Hauppauge. On the left in front stood the gristmill, the second structure was the sawmill, and the third building on the left was the fulling mill added in 1827. When the new Presbyterian Church was constructed in 1827, the old church building was moved to the Mill Pond site and became the fulling mill. The miller's house, on the right, was constructed sometime around 1803. R. S. Feather, 1910, collection of the author

MILLS

Industry came to Smithtown early in its history. While the first occupation of the Smiths was agriculture, the real indication of progress in any town was the construction of a gristmill. The first mill built in town was raised on the east side of the Nissequogue River, north of Landing Avenue bridge, sometime before 1680. The mill was too small and insufficient to handle the work load, and so it was abandoned within a very few years.

The need for a new mill was strong, and planning was required to insure that the mill was of adequate size. On January 27, 1698, the town agreed that Adam Smith "should have the right to the stream called 'Stony Brook' on condition that he erect a dam and build a good sufficient grist mill and maintain the same." Adam Smith, third son of Richard Smith, built the mill in 1699. It was rebuilt after a fire in the early 1800s, and continued to grind commercial flour until the 1940s.

A third mill was constructed at the head of the Nissequogue River between 1700 and 1725. George Phillips, son of the Presbyterian minister at Setauket, erected a gristmill, sawmill and fulling mill. The spillway of the old mill cascades into a wonderful trout holding area known today as White's pool. The mill site is referred to in many old records as the Old Mill or Phillips' Mills.

A fourth mill was constructed twelve years after the end of the Revolutionary War in 1795. Constructed on the property of Caleb Smith, along a stream feeding the Nissequogue River, Willow Pond became the site of a mill built by Paul Theodore Smith, son of Caleb Smith I. After a fire the present mill was reconstructed in 1823.

None of these mills could keep up with increasing demand by the growing population. In 1798 an agreement between Caleb II, Joshua Smith II, and Isaac Blydenburgh resulted in the building of the "new mill" in 1799. The new mill, not to be confused with the old mill near town, was constructed in present-day Blydenburgh Park. The resulting new mill pond was formed on several hundred acres of forest land that had been cut. The waters covered the tree stumps left standing, creating a most noble name, Stump Pond.

This picture from 1900 shows the large mill stone on the left has already been removed. The mill stones were cut and shipped from Connecticut, and brought to docks along the Nissequogue. Today an aging red mill can be seen on the north side of Jericho Turnpike, just back from the entrance to the Caleb Smith State Park. Smithtown Historical Society

Well-preserved stumps submerged for over a hundred years were difficult for workers to remove in 1890. Lures can still be snagged in Old Stump Pond. Smithtown Historical Society

The sawmill cut logs into rough cut lumber. Boards from the Hauppauge mill were used in the construction of homes, barns, and stores throughout Smithtown and Islip. Smithown Historical Society

The New Mill operation at Hauppauge ground corn into flour. Here wagons are unloaded with the grain. The miller received a portion of the milled flour from the customer as payment for his work. It was common in the 1800s for people to pay in goods or services and not in cash money. Smithtown Historical Society

This aerial view shows much of Smithtown's mill history centering around the Nissequogue River. The large pond at the bottom is the millpond of the Blydenburgh Mills, or the New Mills Complex. The next small pond to the north is Vail Pond, then across the road (Jericho Turnpike) is Willow Pond and the mill of Paul Theodore Smith. On the far right, in the upper corner, is the pond created by Phillips' Mills. All of these mills were powered by the Nissequogue River, flowing north to Long Island Sound. Smithtown Historical Society

One hundred three men, including Joseph Blydenburgh, signed the Articles of Association. The vast majority of men in Smithtown stood with the patriot cause against England. This badly eroded headstone can be found in the Hauppauge Methodist Church Cemetery.

CHAPTER 3

The Struggle for Freedom and Independence

THE AMERICAN REVOLUTION

Long Island's role in the American Revolution has been omitted from the pages of American history. Rarely does a name appear that links the residents of Smithtown to that great struggle for freedom and independence. The island was divided along the issue of independence but so was the nation. Benjamin Franklin's son, William, remained a loyalist and became the Royal Governor of New Jersey. The Revolutionary War pitted brother against brother, father against son; its effect on relationships was far greater even than the Civil War. In Smithtown, while Solomon Smith, Daniel Smith, and John L'Homedieu signed the Articles of Association that linked them with the patriot cause, James Smith, Steven Smith, and Jonathan L'Homedieu refused to sign.

In September of 1775 the Provincial Congress assembled in New York and directed the enlistment of militia and the election of officers. The Committees of Huntington, Brookhaven, and Smithtown met to appoint their officers. Most notable was the election of William Floyd of Mastic as colonel, and Edmund Smith Jr. as second major. The muster role of Smithtown's own "minute men" was made on April 7, 1776. The news of fighting at Lexington, Concord, and Bunker Hill crystallized the patriot movement in Suffolk. Many Long Islanders had family ties to Connecticut and Massachusetts. The local militia included Nathaniel Platt, chosen as captain, Samuel Smith, first lieutenant and a long list of sergeants and corporals.

Town government responded to the needs of the new militia, but it was not a priority. Minutes from the town meeting for April 1776, found the following items addressed: the first issue was that no hogs should go on the commons unringed; second, a fence needed to be set and maintained on Long Beach to hold grazing animals; third, soft clams in Stony Brook Harbor shall be farmed and sold to Lemuel Smith for four pence per bushel;

The Platt family were true Smithtown Patriots who fought bravely and suffered greatly at the hands of the British. Zepaniah had four sons who fought in the Revolution. Richard Platt was described by historian William S. Pelletreau as "one of the bravest officers of the Revolution." The Platt portrait, painted by renowned British artist Joseph Wright, was created about 1790. By that time the Platt family found Smithtown much too crowded. The family journeyed to a remote area in upstate New York, later to be aptly named Plattsburgh. Joseph Wright, artist, Smithtown Historical Society

Caleb Smith's house was constructed in 1750. The old house has seen major additions and alterations over the last 250 years. The estate became the home of the Brooklyn Gun Club in 1872, then the Wyandanch Club in 1893. In 1963 the Club was acquired by New York State and is now part of the Caleb Smith State Park. Tony Jerome, Smithtown Historical Society

and fourth, bayonets and cartouch boxes to hold cartridges were to be provided for the militia. Smithtown, poised on the verge of revolution, the Declaration of Independence a mere five months before, continued to consider agricultural affairs more pressing than the affairs of war. News of the Declaration reached Smithtown on July 11, 1776. The townspeople learned that William Floyd had signed for Suffolk County in a call for independence. Floyd stood with Hancock, Jefferson, Adams, Lee, and Franklin to pledge to each other "our lives, our fortunes and our sacred honor."

After the loss of the Battle of Long Island in August 1776, the entire island was occupied by the British Army. Smithtown was under military rule. There were no elections, no judges, no courts of civil judicature. People could not venture to and from New York City without a permit. The prices of farm produce and firewood were regulated by military proclamation. Horses, wagons, provisions could be impressed into the service of the King. Houses were occupied by troops without compensation. The British made residents sign the "Oath of Allegiance to the Crown." It was a forced allegiance and many made the oath only to protect their family and property.

One person who refused to take the Oath of Allegiance to King George III was Caleb Smith I. A graduate of Yale in 1744 and a well-to-do resident, he refused to leave the island as the British invaded. He continuously refused the oath even after being subjected to the most grievous indignities. Caleb was whipped with "hickory gads" and shot at repeatedly. On one occasion, he faced a cutlass wielding British officer who slashed at him, only to miss, leaving a large gash in his front door. The house still bears the scars of the sword and the British occupation.

In December 1777 the British came to the home of Zephaniah Platt who lived on two thousand acres along the banks of Sunken Meadow Creek. Platt, who was seventy-two years of age, was chained to an elm tree in his yard, charged with aiding Patriot raiding parties. The soldiers burned several of Zephaniah's boats and drove off his cattle and livestock. He was arrested and placed on the dreaded prison ships on Wallabout Bay in Brooklyn. Platt's daughter, Dorothea, sought his release from Sir Henry Clinton. The release was granted, but it came too late. Zephaniah had contracted small pox while in prison and died four days after returning home. The Platt family probably had been aiding the rebel cause. The strategic location of their home helped supply whaleboat raiders whose job it was to confuse and harass the British. Although Zephaniah did not die in a major battle, his patriotic efforts were no less great.

The Presbyterian Church in this 1878 photo was not the church of Reverend Joshua Hart. His church, built in 1675, had been a small meetinghouse that originally stood near the junction of Moriches and River Roads. There the church remained until 1825. The church of Joshua Hart was removed to the New Mill site in Hauppauge and the present church, seen here, was dedicated in 1827. G. B. Brainard, 1878, Society for the Preservation of Long Island Antiquities

William Arthur lived in this house built at 315 Middle Country Road about 1750. An early patriot in the struggle for independence, William remained in Smithtown during the British occupation of 1776 to 1783. The house saw numerous additions through the 1850s before it was demolished in the late 1960s. Smithtown Historical Society

Other Smithtown residents held out against the British. Reverend Joshua Hart of the Presbyterian Church spoke out publicly against "the tyranny of Kings" and the lawless acts of the oppressors. A graduate of Princeton, Reverend Hart warned the British not to interfere with the rights of free men. He spoke eloquently from the pulpit; "Beat your plowshares into swords and your pruning shears into spears and let the weak say I am strong. Liberty sounds pleasant in the ears of all mankind and neither men nor devils have the right to tyrannize it over other men." Reverend Hart's sermons infuriated the occupying British. He was arrested numerous times, usually warned and released. One time, however, he was jailed in New York City from May until October 1777, over six months, to teach him a lesson. During his imprisonment, he fell ill and was near death. A fellow prisoner, Colonel Ethan Allen, captured years earlier at Ticonderoga, cared for the ailing Reverend Hart. The minister recovered and was released only to take up exactly where he left off. Enraged beyond description, two British soldiers at once went to the door of the old church and fired at Hart as he was delivering a sermon from the pulpit. Intentional or not, the musket balls missed their mark.

In November of 1778, a final indignity was paid to Reverend Hart. British Lieutenant Colonel Banastre Tarleton carried 6,396 board feet of lumber from the church. Tarleton and his legion spent only four days in Smithtown, but during that time his gross excesses and cruelty were well documented. Not all incidents in the town during the war were so solemn and depressing. William Arthur raised cattle and poultry at his farm on Middle Country Road. One night after learning that the British were camped nearby, Arthur moved to protect his prize ducks from the expected raid for food and supplies. Arthur locked a good number of ducks in his root cellar, hoping that the British would not find them. The next morning, after the British failed to make any demands, William went to check his cellar. To his amazement the majority of his ducks were motionless on the floor, others walked as if infected by some form of motion sickness. Arthur soon realized that his ducks had, somehow, pulled the bung out of his hard cider barrel stored in the cellar. His ducks were not dead, but dead drunk. "Stewed Duck" or "Duck with a Glaze" took on a new meaning in Smithtown's war for independence.

Another colorful incident involved a failure to communicate that benefited Jacob Wheeler, a Hauppauge resident. When the British came to Smithtown, they demanded the surrender of most cattle, hogs, and sheep. Wheeler, like many other residents, had kept his animals penned in a hollow glacial depression along Kings Highway, known as "York Lots." When a group of British soldiers came to Wheeler to demand the surrender of his animals, Wheeler responded, honestly, that they were in "York." Thinking that other troops had already removed the animals to New York City, the soldier left.

The "great oak tree" stood until the late 1950s when it blew down during a severe wind storm. The Abner Smith house, severely altered compared to its 1770 appearance, still stands on the east side of Route 111. Smithtown Historical Society

Not all revolutionary stories involved the men of Smithtown as there were patriot ladies as well. Nancy Smith, daughter of Abner Smith (1734–1782), was in her early teens when the British occupied the town. She was a staunch patriot as was her father, who had signed the Articles of Association and had become a Fourth Sergeant in the Smithtown militia.

The Revolution raged on for seven long years. No other area suffered more under the British occupation than did Long Island. The British had placed a fort in Smithtown, along the sound near Treadwells Neck. The fortification was named Fort Slongo, for the British engineer who designed it. It was the easternmost fortification on the north shore. In October 1781 Fort Slongo played an important part in the end of the Revolution. General Washington was preparing to seize General Cornwallis' troops at Yorktown, Virginia. The British were preparing a fleet in New York City to rescue the trapped British Army. General Washington needed to delay the fleet in New York. He believed that an attack on Fort Slongo would be just the diversion to accomplish the task.

The fort was built high above the bluffs on Treadwells Neck on a farm owned by William Arthur. The Smithtown fortification had a commanding view of Long Island Sound. On Saturday night, October 2, 1781, whaleboat raiders set out from Connecticut. One hundred men, their oarlocks wrapped in leather to muffle any noise, rowed across the sound to Crab Meadow Beach. Upon arriving at the property of Nathaniel Skidmore, the men moved into position and the attack commenced in the early hours of Sunday morning. The majority of British officers were still celebrating the weekend at an inn about a mile away. Other members of the garrison had been dealing with the effects of extra rum rations on Saturday night. The raiders caught the fort unaware. The bleary-eyed British raced into the woods without

British soldiers were in the habit of making camp under a great canopy of oak trees that grew along Hauppauge Road across from the Abner Smith House. One day as the troops were roasting a calf, one of the young British soldiers had the notion to invite young Nancy Smith to share in the meal. "I'll see you in hell first," she replied. Nathan Hale could not have responded any better. The outspoken girl must have startled the redcoats, but they were clear about Nancy's political sympathies.

Although not a forceful patriot, widow Ruth Blydenburgh knew how to take care of herself in a crisis. One evening when thirty British soldiers appeared at her door demand-ing food and drink, she played the role of the poor widow. "Lordy me," she exclaimed, "don't come to a poor lone widow, go over to Netus's (Epenetus Smith) yonder, there's plenty there." And so they did, arriving at the Epenetus Smith Tavern a few minutes later. Smithtown Historical Society

much of a fight. Twenty soldiers were captured, along with a cannon and small arms. The fort was burned with a large supply of cordwood that was destined to be shipped to New York City. The attack was an unqualified success for the Patriot cause. The British were shocked and surprised. Confused by the bold raid, the rescue fleet was delayed. Sir Henry Clinton believed that this might be a prelude to a major assault on New York City. The delay was all Washington needed.

Eleven days later the British army, under General Cornwallis, surrendered in Yorktown. The British band broke in a mournful rendition of an old English song, "The World Turned Upside Down." The victory was the last and greatest action of the war. The victory in Virginia was secured by the efforts of a few who engaged the enemy in a small fort in Smithtown. The end of the Revolutionary War officially came two years later, in 1783, with the Treaty of Paris. In that same year, Smithtown was given town status by the State of New York. The new town was asked to help shoulder the $37,000 tax imposed on Long Island. The State of New York had ruled that Smithtown, along with all of Long Island, had not fought hard enough for independence. Sometimes, in life, there is no justice.

THOMAS TREDWELL

The formal end of the Revolutionary War brought no simple solutions to the new nation. Thomas Tredwell of Sunken Meadow had been an energetic patriot in the conflict. Now he sought to shape the new government as well. He was a member of the New York State Constitutional Convention in 1777; he became a State Senator and a member of the fifty-seven man convention to review the newly proposed Federal Constitution of 1787.

Although we look at the Constitution today as a marvelous document, not everyone in 1787 agreed that it was. John Hancock whose signature on the Declaration of Independence is most striking, questioned the formation of a new national government. Patrick Henry who said, "Give me liberty or give me death," also spoke the not so famous words, "I think I smell a rat," when it came to ratifying the new constitution. The great Henry Lee of Virginia and Governor George Clinton of New York both believed "elected despotism" would ruin the newly won liberty of the states. Smithtown's own Thomas Tredwell feared the creation of big government with national powers. Thomas Tredwell voted his conscience in an extremely bitter battle over the United States Constitution. Riotous disturbances broke out all over New York and Long Island. In the end, the New York Convention ratified the new constitution in a close vote, 30 to 27. Although part of the minority view, Thomas Tredwell added balance to the debate. He was one of the voices that helped shape the new nation.

Thomas Tredwell, J. Albert, artist

WASHINGTON

The Constitution was ratified and the election of the national leaders was complete. General George Washington, the esteemed war hero, was unanimously chosen president of the new United States in 1789. On April 30, 1789, a somewhat nervous Washington took the oath of office on a crowded balcony overlooking Wall Street, in the first capital of the United States, New York City. Almost one year later, President George Washington took a five-day tour of the Long Island countryside. Starting in Brooklyn, the president's gold and cream colored carriage pulled by four matching gray horses surveyed the land as far east as Setauket.

On April 23, 1790, after leaving Setauket, President Washington journeyed down North Country Road, coming into Smithtown from the east. He stopped at the intersection of North Country and Middle Country Roads. His diary simply states, "we baited the horses at Smith's Town at a widow Blydenburgh, a decent house, 10 miles from Setauket." Smithtown residents can't say George Washington "slept here," but they can say he "stepped here." The Blydenburgh house stood at the present site of the Smithtown Library. The house had fallen into disrepair and was torn down in the 1930s. The porch stone that sat in front of the Blydenburgh home now sits as the rear porch stone at the Caleb Smith house, the headquarters of the Smithtown Historical Society. There are not many villages or towns in America that can lay claim to a visit by the first president, George Washington. Smithtown is one of the lucky ones.

WAR OF 1812

The year 1800, marked the turn of a new century. Smithtown life remained largely unchanged even though the spread of commercial agriculture would soon launch a revolution in farm productivity. The Nissequogue River was still the link to the outside world. The accelerated pace of westward expansion created a new, exuberant spirit of opportunity. The Louisiana Purchase of 1803 doubled the size of the United States and the feeling of an infant nationalism was alive in Smithtown, which by that time was almost 150 years old. Town life still shaped people's lives, and there was a good chance, in 1800, that those people who were born in Smithtown would die there. Social ideas and expectations were changing. There was an emphasis on youthfulness, social equality, and individualism that would shape American attitudes in years to come. The election of Thomas Jefferson to the presidency in 1800 and James Madison in 1808 spelled the end of real Federalist control in Washington. A conflict was simmering with England that would soon boil over into war once again.

The War of 1812 was the first war that America fought as a nation. From the very start, the eastern seaboard and Long Island were thrust into the conflict. British warships cruised Long Island Sound and the eastern port of Sag Harbor. Everyone in Smithtown expected an invasion of Long Island similar to the one in 1776. No one looked forward to another round of British occupation. After declaration of war with England, general orders were sent to Captain John Vail of Smithtown. He was instructed to gather the local militia at the "house of Thomas Halliock (Hallock), inn keeper in Smithtown, on Monday, July 26, at 9 o'clock, in the morning." Troops were ordered to march to Sag Harbor for defense of that port. The men were asked to have "cartridge boxes filled, nap sack and blanket, with three days provisions." Lieutenant Alexander Smith, Pratt Wheeler, John Hurtt, John Ketcham, Ebenezer Smith, Jesse Payne, John Darling, Richard Wheeler, L'Homidue (sic) Mills, and others were ordered to prepare for what they expected would be a British invasion by early August. A letter from William Woodhull to John Vail, dated August 27, 1813, set the stage.

To John Vail, August 27, 1813
To say that peace and tranquility prevailed on this part of the island, or in this place particularly would be to subvert the truth—one day we are threatened and expect an invasion from the enemy who is daily parading with their ships in sight of us and the next have enough to do to regulate the effects of whiskey among ourselves. . . .
The enemy lies daily with 2, 3, 4 ships in sight of us, they are continually moving around with their boats from Oyster Ponds to Gardiners Island to Montauk. They sent a boat the other night to the eastward of us and took one penny out of his bed, and carried him a prisoner on board. . . .

William Woodhull

An attempt to take Sag Harbor was made by Commodore T. H. Hardy of the British Navy but the invasion was repulsed. No other serious assaults were made.

John Darling, a local ship captain engaged in trade between Smithtown and New England ports, was captured by the British but not at Sag Harbor. Stopped by a British man-of-war in Long Island Sound, his cargo of merchandise and crew were impressed by the Crown. John thought that he would be either a prisoner or forced into service aboard the British ship until the war's end. Fortune smiled on Mr. Darling, when after a brief conversation with the British Captain, it was revealed that they were both members of the Society of Freemasons. The British Captain granted Darling and crew their freedom, along with a hundred pound note to compensate him for loss of cargo. Although the note of payment was not sufficient to cover the cargo lost, Darling came home with something more valuable—his freedom.

The war ended in 1815 without either side establishing a clear victory. Of course, the British had attacked Washington and burned the president's house, and a Baltimore lawyer, Francis Scott Key, had written a poem about the fight at Fort McHenry. However, in Smithtown little had changed. The local Smithtown militia returned to their homes and farms. River commerce returned to normal as the British blockade of the coast ended.

1816—THE YEAR WITHOUT A SUMMER

The year following the end of the war proved more difficult than the war itself. Notes left by James Darling reveal that 1816 will be remembered as "the year without a summer." The strangest weather struck the Northeast. Frost covered spring plantings through May and June. There were frozen ponds in August and snow in the first weeks of September 1816. Farmers could not plant food crops essential to survival. The cause of the weird spring and summer weather was believed to have been discovered almost a hundred years later. In 1815 the explosion of two volcanoes, Mount Tambora (Indonesia) and Mount Suferieri, threw so much ash into the atmosphere that an immense cloud drifted around the world, lowering the overall temperatures. Residents of Smithtown did record some strange sunsets during those summer months.

The winter of 1816–17, for most Smithtown families, was difficult at best. All the root cellars were bare. Before the days of refrigerators, freeze-dried fruit and Birdseye frozen vegetables, people lived from harvest to harvest. Amazingly, according to John Darling, only one place was left frost free, a small section of Hauppauge called "Little Egypt." Mary Jane Wheeler, John's wife, had family in Hauppauge and they helped the Darlings through the winter. In the spring of 1817 Smithtown residents faced another crisis. With no harvest in 1816, there was no seed to plant. Neighbors in Hauppauge allowed Smithtown residents one bushel of wheat, rye, oats, and potatoes to plant for the new season. It was good to have friends in Hauppauge.

SMITHTOWN DEBATING SOCIETY

Before the 1820s politics was primarily the business of the social and economic elite. By 1824 many states were removing voter restrictions and the average American became more interested in the issues of his time. America was awash in intellectual change and political reform. Andrew Jackson told America in 1828 that it was time to "purify" and "reform the government." The nation responded and four times more men turned out to vote in the election of 1828 than had in 1824. Smithtown was very much a part of this democratic change. In 1829 a Debating Society was created by four men: S. A. Smith, Charles A. Floyd, George K. Hubbs, and Abraham P. Sherril. Other men joined, engaging in monthly debates on the political and philosophical issues of the day.

What marks the Smithtown Debating Society as unique among others of the nation was the signature of its new recording secretary on December 7, 1837. The signature was that of Walter Whitman, who signed the minutes as just Walt Whitman. This young man, a teacher, was drawn into the debates and issues of the day. The 1837 and 1838 debates included many topics which still give rise to discussion today. "Has nature more influence than education in the formation of character?" "Is the system of slavery as it exists in the South right?" This issue sharply divided the Society, as it would the nation twenty-three years later. The Society voted four to three that slavery was wrong. "Immigration of foreigners should be discouraged." Seven out of ten thought that it should, while Walt voted with the minority. "Capital punishment ought to be abolished in New York," was the question January 17, 1838. The Society voted that it ought not be abolished by five to four, Whitman, again, voting with the minority. Other issues concerned "the treatment of Indians," the question of "Equal education for males and females," "Restricted sale of spirits in town" and "Should taxes be used to support public schools?" The Society met for over twenty years, raising the consciousness of the little rural town to new intellectual heights. Walt Whitman made his last notes as a secretary on March 21, 1838. I often wonder just how much of Walt Whitman's thoughts, perceptions of people, his ideals, and values were shaped by his time in Smithtown, and how much his later work "Leaves of Grass" was nourished by the Debating Society of Smithtown.

The British soldiers arrived at the Smith Tavern located just west of the Presbyterian Church. The service and accommodations must have been excellent. By war's end, the British armies left Epenetus with an unpaid balance of almost 588 English pounds. Epenetus recorded the highest debt owed to anyone in all of Smithtown. To this day that debt remains unpaid.

The open countryside still dominated much of Smithtown in 1878. This view is the landscape near St. Johnland, Kings Park. G. B. Brainard, 1878, Society for the Preservation of Long Island Antiquities

CHAPTER 4

Life in Smithtown

FARMING

Can you imagine a town where the land rolled unbroken for as far as the eye could see? A place where houses only dotted the vista of gently rolling hills and roughly hewn posts with split rails marked the end of a neighbor's property. For most of Smithtown's history, the life and work of the population centered around agriculture. Very little change occurred between 1650 and 1860. The cultivation of crops was a continuous process. First, the land was cleared, timber cut, underbrush burned and the few stones found were cleared away. Stumps from trees were left to rot until they could be uprooted easily.

The land was then planted with crops like wheat, rye, barley, oats, and flax, crops that had made their way to the island from Europe. Common grass was also grown and used as animal feed when salt hay from the marshes had been over harvested. Crops such as peas and beans along with native crops of corn and pumpkins were planted. Daniel Denton's *A Brief Description of New York*, published in 1670, listed the principal crops of Long Island as grain, tobacco, hemp, flax, pumpkins, and melons. Potatoes, which were the primary agricultural product of Long Island in the 1940s, were introduced on Long Island in 1636. There are no records of any significant harvests in Smithtown until the mid 1700s. By that time the small, watery tubers had met with popular approval and appeared on the family menu.

Fruit trees were brought from Europe and planted in small orchards around the farm. Apples were harvested as a popular addition to the fall diet. These wonderfully versatile fruits could be stewed, baked, fried, dried, and made into pies, cakes, or puddings. They could be eaten raw or cooked along with other vegetables. Apples with flaws or bruises that were not storable could be pressed into cider, fermented into apple jack, apple wine, or apple brandy. It is said that Richard Smith planted an orchard around his home in Nissequogue. A pear tree found near his home site produced button pears until 1880. The variety of fruit trees probably included apples, cherries, plums, and pears. Naturally growing fruits like cranberries, mulberries, huckleberries, blackberries, persimmons, grapes, raspberries, and strawberries were harvested as they matured in open meadows and woodlands.

Cattle roam the open pastures at Head of the River in Smithtown. The railroad trestle on the right of this rural scene dates this photo to sometime after 1872, probably closer to 1910. Collection of the author

In the seventeenth and eighteenth centuries, the farmer was also a hunter and a fisherman. Wild game like venison, quail, rabbits, squirrels, and assorted waterfowl were the main source of protein. Freshwater and saltwater varieties of fish along with clams and oysters were also available from the river and harbors in and around town. Several varieties of livestock were introduced to Smithtown by the 1660s. Richard Smith's 1663 tax inventory showed that he owned several lambs, oxen, cows, horses, hogs, and sheep. The domestic animals of the period were more distinguished for their hardiness than for their meat and dairy products. Most animals imported in the early 1600s to Long Island were used to build up the domestic herds and not slaughtered as food sources with any regularity.

Sheep were introduced to Long Island in 1643, and became enormously important to the Smithtown economy in the eighteenth century. The wool sheared from sheep was carded and spun into yarn and then woven into cloth. It started as a small cottage industry, but soon fulling mills, like those constructed at New Mill Pond in Hauppauge and Phillips' Mill at Head of the River, were producing commercial wool. Government purchases of wool from Smithtown began as early as the War of 1812 and continued through the Civil War. Everyone owned a few sheep and, often, the town would allow for common pasturage. In May, after the flocks of sheep were sheared of their precious fleece, they were released into the fields to play out the days of summer. In early November, the sheep were driven off the commons and redistributed to their owners by means of identification marks.

Town meetings were taken up with the recording of ear marks for primary identification of live stock. In 1724 Smithtown records indicate that "Ebenezer Smith's ear mark is a crop of the off ear and a hole of the near ear." At a meeting in November 1736 it was recorded that, "Isaac Jarrett, his ear mark is a 'V' in the left ear." In April 1743, "Samuel Tillison's ear mark is a crop on the right ear and a half penny on the for side of the same, and a latch on the underside of the left." On January 15, 1771, Caleb Smith's mark was listed as, "A crop on off ear and a slope under side the near ear, and a half penny upper side of the slope." One ponders that the development of the short eared variety of domestic animals may have occurred more because of the extensive marking procedure than due to some unique genetic strains.

Hogs were good to have on a Smithtown farm, since they could help the farmer dispose of any edible household garbage. It was obvious that local swine left unattended might find their way to a neighbor's field and root up his crops. In April 1746 the town meeting in Smithtown voted, "that no

The life of the farm laborer was not an easy one. Here, two farm hands work with Morgan Brower Blydenburgh in the processing of several hogs. The hogs have been killed and are now being "scalded." Large quantities of boiling water were used to remove the hair from the hides. Smithtown Historical Society

With the carcasses left hanging to dry, the process of butchering would begin. Fresh pork, smoked hams, bacon, sausage, or scrapple would find their way to the dining table. Nothing was wasted, even the heads of the animals were boiled until the meat dropped off. Then herbs and spices were added to the mixture to make a souse, a pickled meat. Smithtown Historical Society

hogs should go in the common without rings on penalty of paying one shilling per head for every hog that shall be complained of."

Young bulls were often castrated, paired in teams, and trained to work in the fields. Smithtown farmers often preferred oxen power to the luxury of horse power. Even in the 1740s, there was common concern for control of domesticated animals. To protect the salt marsh, the town voted in April 1747 "We should stop horses and cattle from going on the Long Beach and Little Beach by stopping them by fence at Pig Creek."

Farming in Smithtown was a year round activity that called for constant attention to crops and livestock. The farmer worked in sun or rain, and even on weekends animals needed to be fed and watered. There was little leisure time, just time for doing different farm chores. A bad day, one either too cold, too hot, or too rainy, might be turned into a day to go fishing, hunting, raking clams, or setting out traps.

The springtime was full of activity because it meant plowing and planting grain crops and flax. In summer more crops were planted, hay was cut and carted, and sheep sheared. Fall was time for harvest and that process continued until the frost. Rye, corn, and wheat were gathered. Hay and flax were carted. The ground was plowed and harrowed for the winter.

Pumpkins were not just carved for Halloween as they are today; the large orange gourds were harvested and used for food. The hard pumpkin

St. James was still primarily a farming community in the 1890s when this photo of the O'Berry farm was taken. The haying process was in transition between primitive hand operations and the machine age. Here, horses are working on a treadmill supplying the "horse power" via belts, gears, and wheels to the thresher. Steam power, then gasoline engines soon improved the process. Smithtown Historical Society

flesh was cut into pieces and boiled for hours until soft. The pumpkin stew was then flavored with butter and spices. Sometimes combined with cornmeal it could be baked into a bread, or by itself, it might be made into a rich pie. Corn was a native island crop that when harvested was husked, dried, taken off the cob, and ground into a flour or meal. The corn meal was mixed with milk and cooked to make a porridge known as *samp*. A spoon bread, or ash cake, was made by combining corn meal with water or animal fat, then cooking it over hot ashes in the fire.

Cords of wood were cut, chopped, and cured before being used as fuel for winter. Winter would be long and the warmth of a house was measured by the sweat of the woodcutter. Homes were almost as cold as the outdoors in winter or hotter than the outdoors in summer. Coal did not become a regular fuel source until the 1890s.

Winters were spent repairing farm tools and machinery or building furniture. Animals still needed to be fed and dung removed from the barns and carted away. The process of rotting or retting of flax might be finished in the winter months. Bundles of flax were made ready for spinning. Women used a drop spindle or spinning wheel to twist the long line flax fibers into thread. From the term *line flax*, we get the word *linen*. Linen threads would be woven into cloth, and women would spend the winter months making and repairing clothes for the next year. The Smithtown farmer, his wife and children worked hard from dawn to dusk, week after week.

When people speak of returning to the "good old days," they should think again about those "good old days." Most work was hard and dirty. Pots were made of cast iron, were heavy, and not easily cleaned. Food was preserved by canning, drying, salting, or storing in an icehouse in the days before refrigerators. To wash clothes, water had to be drawn from a well or carried from the creek and heated in a large caldron in the yard. Clothes were put in, stirred in the boiling water, and then thrown over lines or bushes to dry. Food was cooked over open fires or roasted on hand-turned spits. All of this work was hard and was done by hand. After spending a very long day performing the tasks of a nineteenth-century farmer at Smithtown Heritage Day, the author's son once said, "The good old days were not that good; the people must have died young."

EDUCATION

In New York in the 1700s the school system as we know it today did not exist. The majority of children in the state never saw the inside of a schoolroom in their young lives. Some children attended private academies, and others attended church schools. The cost of these private facilities made schooling a luxury that many people could not afford. Governor George Clinton urged the establishment of public schools as early as 1782. However, it was only in 1795 that the state legislature passed an experimental act to establish schools with the help of public funds. The aid was intended only for the payment of teachers' salaries, and nothing more. Smithtown's portion of that first education fund was 61.5 pounds per year. The experiment was short-lived and ended by 1799.

The first known schoolhouse in Smithtown was private and built on land owned by Epenetus Smith II. The school was a simple one-room structure located on the north side of Main Street, west of the Presbyterian Church. The Articles of Association for the purpose of erecting the school were entered into on January 27, 1802. People who wanted their children to attend school purchased shares in the school association. Records indicate that Thomas Arthur purchased two shares in 1802 for ten dollars each. Initially, the goal of private education was to teach only the basics, which included the "three R's Read'n', 'Rit'n', and 'Rithmetic." It was obvious, early on, that spelling must also be included to complete the basic educational needs.

In 1804 a similar association was formed in Hauppauge. Shares were sold and a small school house was built on the land of Caleb Smith II. In Nissequogue a school had been in existence prior to 1808. Documents

Smithtown's first school, known also as the Whitman School House, is now located on Singer Lane, south of Main Street. R. S. Feather, collection of the author

Head of the River School was a private school built sometime before 1804 on "Timmy's lot," north of New Mill Road. After the Civil War, the school was moved to the north side of Meadow Road, just past the intersection of Jericho Turnpike. Today, it is a private residence. R. S. Feather, Smithtown Historical Society

Commack North, circa 1890, was one of the two Commack schools available to the people as a result of the Common School Act of 1812. Situated on Townline Road at the end of the Methodist Cemetery, it had originally been a private school academy before becoming a public facility. Smithtown Historical Society

indicate that in 1808 the school was moved to a location that proved inconvenient to subscribers at the time. A new school was proposed, but subscriptions were not sufficient to pay for its construction. Eight residents in the area contributed money in varying amounts "so that the burden would not fall on one or two" and so that each contributor would have the right to "school his children." The idea of sharing an educational burden was voiced in the Nissequogue area. People were seeing the need for and benefit of a collective educational system.

Less than four years later, in 1812, the state legislature passed an act for the establishment of public schools. No aid would be paid out, however, until the education fund reached $50,000. The act provided for state aid, but also called for local taxation to raise additional funds. The law required the selection of local school commissioners and trustees to oversee educational affairs.

By January 1814 public education became part of Smithtown life. Eleven school districts were designated by the town. Over the next fourteen years, new districts emerged; some were combined and others vanished altogether. By 1828 the first record of the town's school districts was made. It listed fourteen districts with a total of 540 pupils. The length of the school year varied from school to school, with each district exerting a great deal of independence. Some districts met a mere three months while others held school for as much as twelve months. Most districts, however, met between three and six months under the direction of "approved" teachers.

By 1816, just after the end of the War of 1812, the private little schoolhouse of Smithtown was purchased by the village for $500 and open to any child of Smithtown. State funds along with local tax money were combined to pay most school costs. Still, the schools were not free. If parents could not pay the school fees, they had to sign a pauper's oath admitting that they had no funds for education. Some Smithtown residents were too proud to sign any oath admitting to poverty, so their children did not attend. Since education, while publicly supported, was not mandatory, some parents preferred to have their children at home to help with farm chores. Other students attended school only infrequently.

Probably the best known facility of the nineteenth century was the Little School House in Smithtown, located on Main Street. It was there, in 1837–38, that Walt Whitman, at the ripe old age of nineteen, was instructing Smithtown's youth. In the small, one-room building, Walt worked with a variety of ages and abilities. The school itself was unpainted inside and out. A small wood stove raised the interior temperature slightly

Minnie Van Brunt's Class of 1912 poses for their class portrait. In the top row, from left to right, are: Jeffrey Smith, Ed Hubbs, Eva Cunningham, teacher Minnie Van Brunt, George Robbins, Annie Hunt, Ruth Burr, Mattie Smith, Frances Ketcham, and Addie Robbins. In the middle row are: Daisy Sammis, Mabel Wicks, Pearl Dezendorf, Mabel Wood, Mildred Wood, Huldah Whitman, Emma Burr, Annie Goldsmith, Angie Robbins, Grace Robinson, Stella Richmond, Grace Smith, Grace Burr, and Adeline Robinson. In the front row are: George Sammis, Charles Kahrs, Frederick Goldsmith, Tunis Burr, Lester Burr, Paul Goldsmith, Fred Ketcham, Clarence Smith, and Charles Conklin. Mrs. Van Brunt also helped to establish Commack's first Public Library. Smithtown Historical Society

above freezing in the winter. Parents of pupils carted wood to school, where older boys would cut it and younger lads would carry the cut pieces inside. There were no matches and often students had to go to B. E. Blydenburgh's house or "Uncle" Epenetus Smith's for a brand of fire to start the stove. The girls were required to sweep and clean the schoolroom once a week and occasionally scrub it down. There were no indoor plumbing facilities and other accommodations were bleak. The seats were hard and uncomfortable; there were neither maps nor a blackboard to aid instruction. Papers and pencils were scarce. Students often wrote on small slate boards with chalk. Pens were goose quills sharpened and split by the teacher with his small "pen knife." If you used a pen you brought your own quill and your own ink, too. There were no state

Commack South was the second school built to accommodate students from the Commack area, circa 1910. Collection of Joel Streich

funds for school supplies or lunches. The teacher might be forced to board with the families of students in town. Walt Whitman was known to have stayed at the Hallock Inn, then later with the Conklin family. Mrs. Conklin reported that teacher Whitman had only one shirt. She used to wash it every night and have it ironed and ready for him in the morning.

Education in the early part of the nineteenth century was a trial for both teacher and students. Backers of a totally free school system fought hard to convince parents that democracy needed educated voters to work effectively. Finally, in the reform period following the Civil War, the State of New York ruled that all public schools would be free to all students. Supported by state and local tax money, the schoolhouse door was now open to everyone without additional fees. Shortly after the state ruling, on April 4, 1868, Smithtown took action and, by a vote of twenty-three to two, agreed to set up Smithtown's Union Free School District No. 1. Lyman Beecher Smith, Judge Lawrence Smith, Daniel A. Smith, William E. Newton, and Elijah Brush were elected to the first Board of Education. This action was taken in order to take advantage of the generosity of one man—Jonas Smith. Known to local residents as "Rich Jonas," the wealthy ship owner from Stony Brook left $8000 in his will for the "cause of education at

The first school in St. James was in the hollow on Three Sisters Road. Over ninety scholars were in attendance around 1905. In the 1920s this building became the Bohemia Social Club, a part of the Actors' Colony. R. S. Feather, 1905, collection of Richard and Marie Sturm

The St. James Elementary School on North Country Road was built in 1908–1909, at a total cost of $7,500. Students who completed studies in St. James could now walk for over an hour each day to attend high school classes in Smithtown. This landmark building was rescued and restored in the 1990s. Converted to commercial office space, it is an excellent example of adaptive reuse of historic structures. R. S. Feather, 1920; Gift of Dorothy Hiller Otto, Smithtown Historical Society

Smithtown Branch." It was as he said, "my intention in the bequest to lay the foundation of an educational institution in said village which shall confer the greatest on the greatest numbers." The Board, acting under Jonas Smith's request, purchased land on Main Street west of the Presbyterian Church. The original "little school house" was sold for $200 and moved south of Main Street on what is today called Singer Lane. In 1869 builder

The Kings Park schoolroom of a Mr. Appleby was photographed in 1905; the schoolroom was located on Old East Northport Road. In the back row, from left to right, are: Joe McDonald, unknown, unknown, John Hyland (?), and Allen Smith. In the middle row are: Mabel Fields, Bill Fields, Bill Sheridan, unknown, unknown, unknown, and Maggie Dunn. In the front row are: Nellie Warren, Nelson Nichols, Florence Keitel, Florence Walker, May Koltr, and Lillian Conklin. King Peddler Collection, Smithown Historical Society

Hauppauge schoolchildren, circa 1906. Collection of the author

Built in 1869, the Academy was locat-ed just west of the Presbyterian Church on Main Street. Collection of the author

The new school was constructed around 1907 on Old Dock Road where the present William T. Rogers Junior High School is located. After graduation, eighth grade students would attend either Northport or Smithtown High School. By 1928 the total enrollment of Kings Park Schools was 250 and the teaching staff numbered only eight individuals. Kings Park Heritage Museum Collection

Peter Jayne constructed "an academy" for a total cost of $5800 paid out of Smith's grant. A plaque, in the memory of Jonas Smith and his wife Nancy, was hung in the new school. That building served the educational needs of Smithtown for many years.

Almost forty years later residents of Smithtown met on a cool evening in May 1908 to vote on a new eight-room frame building. The vote was fairly close, forty-nine to thirty-four, but construction of a "new school" at a cost of $12,762 was approved. Built by Everett Hand, the 1910 building was bigger and better than the last. The school was complete with all modern conveniences, central heating with a coal boiler, electric lighting and even a school bell in an appropriate bell tower. The old academy was sold for $536.56 and moved west on Main Street where it was used as a commercial establishment. An additional one-half acre of property was purchased behind the new academy in 1915.

In 1918 Frank E. Brush was elected clerk of the Smithtown School District; a position he would hold for the next thirty years. It was obvious that educational services in Smithtown needed to expand. The growing population called for more classrooms, teachers, and improved facilities. In 1923 portable buildings were added for $3000. These additions were still

Hauppauge constructed a new school in the post-Civil War period. The new 1866 building was located on School House Lane. Postcard, collection of Mr. Bud Land

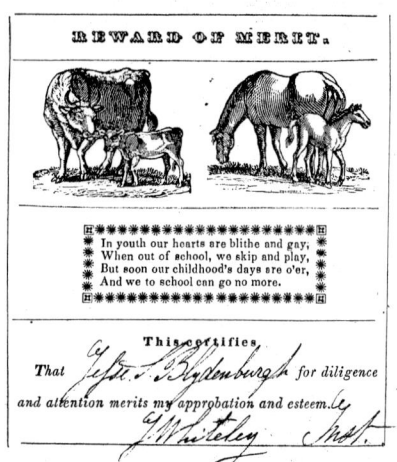

Report cards and progress notes are not new to the education process. Jesse Blydenburgh must have loved getting this report from his teacher, a Mr. Whitely. Smithtown Historical Society

inadequate to meet the growing needs. On June 2, 1924, by an overwhelming vote of sixty-six to thirteen, a proposition was passed to authorize a bond issue of $260,000 for a new elementary and high school building. A ten-acre site was chosen opposite the railroad station and purchased from Francis Smith for $30,000. The new school was constructed on New York Avenue. Smithtown had come a long way from the days of its first one-room schoolhouse.

AFRICAN AMERICAN HISTORY

African American history begins in 1619 with the first introduction of slaves to Jamestown, Virginia. A short time later, in 1626, the Dutch introduced the same institution to a willing and receptive English population here on Long Island. While we often think of slavery as an exclusively Southern institution, that is not the case. In 1700 New York State had a greater population of slaves than did the state of Virginia. Smithtown black history begins in the seventeenth century. Richard Smith owned at least two black slaves. In his will of 1692, the patentee disposed of his property. He "bequeathed" two slaves to his two sons, Richard and Job.

The New School in Smithtown, 1910. R. S. Feather, Smithtown Historical Society

Smithtown Branch High School, 1924. Postcard published by G. D. Marsh, collection of the author

At a school celebration, possibly Arbor Day activities, a tree is being planted on the right, circa, 1911. R. S. Feather, Gift of Dorothy Hiller Otto, Smithtown Historical Society

The spring of 1928 found the Smithtown Branch High School Baseball Team posed proudly on the steps of the New York Avenue building. The crash of Wall Street was a little more than a year away. A long hard depression and a world war lay ahead for these young boys from Smithtown. In the top row, from left to right, are: John Faxon, Coach Pearsall, Edward W. Kozlik, Clinton Spahr, George Kerr, and Robert Germond. In the bottom row are: John Flynn, Arthur Kozlik, Nick Micciche, Rudy Johnson, Floyd Sanford, Arthur Stiffel, and unknown. Edward W. Kozlik, photographer, Smithtown Historical Society

School sports became part of education after the turn of the century. Additional courses and athletic activities became more varied during the Roaring Twenties. The Smithtown Girls' Basketball Team of 1924–25 finished third in the league that year. Miss Byers, the coach, is standing on the right. Players include in the bottom row, from left to right: Anna Ruck, Ruth Hase, Dorothy Coombs, Gertrude Woobenhorse, and Ruth Crane. In the top row are: Madeline Cordes, Edna Peterson, Ruth Purick, and Coach Byers. Smithtown Historical Society

A painting by Stony Brook artist Shepard A. Mount dates from the 1830s. It marks an important change in the status of African Americans in New York State. In 1827 with a sweep of the pen Governor Clinton ended the institution of slavery in New York State. This portrait simply labeled "Tamer" catches a faint smile of a young woman. Smithtown records indicate a young slave girl named "Tamer" had been sold on February 12, 1800. John Smith bartered Tamer for $225 to William and Richard Blydenburgh. By 1830, however, Tamer was a free woman. Both Shepard A. Mount and his brother, William S. Mount, are well known for their careful portrayal of African American life on Long Island. Oil portrait, private collection

A "Negro Harry" and his "Negro Robin" were handed down from one generation to the next. What is amazing is that, in the same document, Richard sees fit to grant manumission to one of the slaves. Richard states, "Negro Robin is bequeathed for ye term of twelve years and at ye end of said twelve years the said Robin shall be free." In this early document questions are raised about the early relationship between owners and slaves. Why did Richard provide for the freedom of one slave and not the other? What was the personal or family relationship between "Negro Harry" and "Negro Robin"? Did Richard see, at an early date, the need of black emancipation? Was this the act of a progressive thinker or just a response to loyalty shown to him by a servant? These questions may never be adequately answered.

The census of June 1776, just one month before the formal Colonial Declaration of Independence, showed a total population in Smithtown of 716 persons, 161 of whom were of African descent. It is not indicated in the census how many African Americans were free, and how many were slaves. It is presumed that "Robin" had been set free by this time, but whether he or she still lived in Smithtown is not known. Out of forty-four families in Smithtown, thirty-eight families owned slaves. The two largest slaveholders were Thomas Tredwell and Edmund Smith Jr., each of whom owned twelve slaves.

The African American population of Smithtown helped to build the country with their labor, as did slaves everywhere. In 1788 the slave code in New York State was changed to permit slave owners to free slaves if the person freed was in good health and less than fifty years of age. The first documented emancipation in Smithtown came when Thomas Tredwell freed "Charles" in "consideration of the fidelity and past services." By 1800 the trend toward voluntary manumission had begun to take shape. There were 165 slaves in Smithtown, but eighty-six African Americans were now listed as "free persons." Gradually the total of free blacks increased until July 4, 1827, when slavery ended in New York State.

It is believed that sometime between 1825 and the early 1900s, former slaves met to discuss common problems in Smithtown. Although freedom was the most important issue of the day, it was not the only issue. The problems of economic survival and discrimination in civil and social codes did not vanish with the end of slavery. The issues of society and common Christian faith bonded African Americans together. The location of these early meetings was on property owned by the Smith family. Today this area is near the intersections of New York Avenue and Wildwood Lane.

The black servants' quarters of Caleb Smith II in Commack date from the nineteenth century. Although the main house was saved, this small outbuilding was demolished in 1955. Library of Congress, Smithtown Historical Society

The gatherings in the woods became more formal with the construction of a church in 1910. Although the church was built in the twentieth century, there is good evidence of the A.M.E. Church in Smithtown long before that date. In the *History of Long Island*, by Nathaniel Prime, 1845, the author states that Smithtown and Islip had an African Methodist Episcopal (A.M.E.) (Zion) Church Society of twenty-five members. It is known that Setauket had a society as early as 1815, yet did not construct a church until 1874. The Bethel A.M.E. of Huntington had a Society in 1843. It is safe to say that Smithtown's society began before 1845, but the exact date is not known.

The A.M.E. church was founded by Richard Allen, a former slave, in the exact same year, 1787, and the exact same city, Philadelphia, as the United States Constitution. The A.M.E. Church of Smithtown was built in a simple style, one room with a small coal stove for heat. The exterior had brown cedar shingles, no steeple or bell. In August of 1931 the Smith family, specifically Isadora Smith, transferred the property to the congregation for one dollar. The church land was finally freed through the generosity of one the patentee's descendants. In 1990 the church members celebrated the anniversary of the only church in Smithtown ever organized by African Americans.

Sometime around the year 1830 Epenetus Smith (1760–1832) found a young runaway slave from Maryland alone and afraid in New York City. The young African American, named Garnet, had escaped the harsh conditions of a Southern plantation only to find hunger and poverty in the North. Epenetus took the young boy back to Smithtown, not as a slave, but as a ward. Garnet stayed in Smithtown and became a close friend of Epenetus' son, Samuel Arden. Both boys attended school together, worked together, and enjoyed life in Smithtown. The Smith family was impressed with Garnet's fine intelligence and wit. They realized that he was capable of greater learning and opportunities outside of Smithtown.

The Smith family sent Garnet, a free man, off to New England and on to college studies. Graduating with high honors, Garnet went to Troy, New York, to join the ministry of a Presbyterian Church. Reverend Hervey Highland Garnet, D.D., emerged, not only as a minister, but an advocate for the national abolition of slavery in America. The memories of his own youth as a runaway slave drove him to action. His strong and eloquent speeches drew crowds wherever he went. Garnet was selected to attend the World's Antislavery Convention at Exter Hall in London, England. He remained in Europe for several years preaching against the "peculiar" American institution. Returning to America, he took over the ministry of the thirteenth Presbyterian Church

The tintype portrait is simply labeled "Charles Dobbs Smithtown 1880." His age indicates a man who had seen the end of the Civil War, the passage of the Thirteenth, Fourteenth, and Fifteenth Amendments to the Constitution. Freedom, citizenship, and suffrage were granted by law; equality would be won in a struggle to last the next hundred years. Richard H. Handley Collection, Long Island Room, Smithtown Library

Trinity A.M.E. Church, New York Avenue, Smithtown. Photograph by the author

In 1888 the class of the Head of the River School posed for their picture. The pupils of Essie Brush's class were not restricted by age, sex, or color. Smithtown Historical Society

By 1898 a few black families in Smithtown had acquired property. However, most individuals were still listed on the census as laborers, servants, boat hands, or farmers. In this photo, a traditional job of loading a wagon with thatch cut from the river is being accomplished at the common crossing on Jericho Turnpike, close to the bull today. Queens Borough Public Library, Long Island Collection

in Washington, D.C., just as the Civil War was drawing near. He became acquainted with the new president, Abraham Lincoln, and soon became his trusted confidant. In 1863 Abraham Lincoln, with the urging of Reverend Garnet, issued the Emancipation Proclamation.

The War Between the States was now a moral war to end the institution of slavery. The following year, in 1864, the president asked that there be an anniversary observance of the Proclamation. Reverend Garnet was chosen orator of the day by unanimous choice of the President, Vice-President Andrew Johnson, the Cabinet, and the chaplains of both houses of Congress. The runaway slave, rescued and nurtured in Smithtown, had risen to become the first African American to speak before the House of Representatives.

In a little more than a year, the Civil War was over and Lincoln was dead. The world of the African American was forever changed. Some of that change was instituted with the help of Reverend Garnet. A brilliant life emerged from the darkness of slavery. A family from Smithtown had helped a young man reach his potential. Two boys from Smithtown had worked and played together, each blind to the difference in their color. Reverend Garnet and Samuel Arden Smith, although separated by many miles, remained good friends for the remainder of their lives.

Shortly after the Civil War, in 1866, the Howard Colored Orphan Asylum was founded by Mrs. Sarah A. Tillman, the widow of an African American pastor in Brooklyn. The Freedman's Bureau and the African Colonization Society helped open the first facility in Manhattan. Much like St. Johnland in Kings Park and Locustdale in Hauppauge, the Howard effort was a product of progressive ideals in the post-Civil War period.

In 1906 property was purchased in St. James. Attempts were made to teach farming skills to African Americans. In 1910 the directors left St. James and purchased the five-hundred-acre Indian Head Farm in Kings Park, changing the name of the facility to the Howard Orphanage and Industrial School. Here students were taught carpentry, sewing, cobbling, typing, and basic skills needed for domestic work or farming. Children were "bound out" to families in the area to learn a trade or skill.

The Howard facility operated until a series of tragic events closed it in 1918. The directors were never able to obtain broad financial backing. Contributions normally made to the orphanage were diverted to the war bond effort. A coal shortage during the severe winter of 1917–1918, caused a number of Howard children to contract frostbite which in some cases resulted in amputation. The children were removed from the facility and transferred to other homes.

Mrs. James Gordon, wife of the superintendent at the Howard Orphanage (1902–1913). This picture was taken in St. James in 1907. Howard Orphanage, Smithtown Historical Society

The innocence of youth is captured as the children of the Treadwell, Smith, and Phillips families pose for a picture at the house of C. T. Emmett in St. James, circa 1900. Smithtown Historical Society

Efforts to save the Howard Orphanage were made by many prominent Smithtown citizens including Morgan Blydenburgh, Mrs. Richard Handley, Miss Cornelia Peek, Mr. Lawrence Smith Butler, Mrs. Charles E. Lawrence, Mrs. Charles A. Miller, Mrs. Prescott H. Butler, Mrs. Edward H. L. Smith, and Mrs. Theodore W. Smith. Charges of racism might be made in other places, but not in Smithtown in 1918. The Howard Orphanage was sadly a financial casualty of the great war.

Mary Emma (Minnie) Mills of Smithtown never knew Reverend Garnet. She had been born after the Civil War on April 15, 1869, four years to the day after Lincoln died at the hands of an assassin. The child of a Shinnecock Indian father and a runaway slave mother, Minnie was born as her mother worked the fields somewhere east of Smithtown. The majority of her days, however, were spent as a Smithtown resident. Minnie worked most of her life as a governess, yet she told stories of delivering vegetables and milk for the Brush Dairy in Huntington. She often spoke of deliveries to President Roosevelt at his home in Oyster Bay. After Mrs. Joseph Dowling of St. James passed away, Minnie was hired to raise the eleven Dowling children. Following her service for Mr. Dowling, she was hired by Hancock Griffin, a lawyer in Smithtown, to look after his six children. When Minnie died at the age of 105, in 1974, the Reverend William Edwards spoke to the people gathered at the First Presbyterian Church and called for "a celebration of the life of Minnie Mills."

The church service was awash in memories as a dozen or so people spoke of her selfless dedication to children, to helping others and to just spreading good cheer for over a hundred years. Up until the age of eighty-seven, she continued to drive her 1926 Model T Ford around Smithtown, often on the wrong side of the road. Smithtown resident Frank Stepanek said that her car paralleled her life, "both were simple, no frills, hard working and long lasting."

In 1959, at the age of ninety, fifteen years before her death, the local NAACP honored her, not for civil rights activism or militancy, but for the great dignity with which she conducted her whole life. Buried in Smithtown Cemetery across from the Presbyterian Church that she attended, a small headstone tells nothing of her life. Yet it was not the color of her skin that people remember, but the extraordinary content of her character that touched and shaped the lives around her.

The Howard Orphanage literature from 1910 labeled this photo "Lots of Baseball."
Howard Orphanage, Smithtown Historical Society

George Lafayette Booth, 1862, 127th New York Volunteers. Tintype, Smithtown Historical Society

CHAPTER 5

Civil War and Change

Abraham Lincoln solemnly took the oath of office on March 4, 1861. He became the president of, not the United States, but the disunited states. Seven states had already seceded from the Union by inauguration day and eight more states teetered on the edge of disunion. Lincoln's inaugural address was conciliatory. There would be no war unless the South initiated the attack.

In March 1861 sentiment on Long Island was to let the Southerners leave the Union quietly. There was no widespread support for freeing all slaves in the South. New York had emancipated its slaves by 1827, but that was a state decision, not a federal one. The 1860 campaign had contained a referendum in New York. Voters were asked to give equal voting rights to "people of color." Although Lincoln won the presidency in New York and carried Suffolk, the referendum for Black Suffrage was defeated. The War Between the States would not start over the issues of "slave and free."

The attack on Fort Sumter in Charleston Harbor on April 12, 1861, polarized Northern sentiment. The North would not tolerate a wanton attack on the flag and its troops. The war would be fought to "protect the Union." The thirty-four-hour bombardment of that Charleston harbor fortress cost no Union lives. However, the war that lay ahead would cost more American lives than the nation would lose in all the wars the United States would fight from the American Revolution through the Vietnam conflict. Smithtown paid its share of the war's cost in dollars and human life.

On April 15, three days after the firing on Fort Sumter, President Lincoln called upon the states of the Union to assist the federal government in suppression of the Southern rebellion. The first request was modest, only seventy-five thousand volunteers would be called to serve a six-month enlistment. The first volunteers were raised in Brooklyn, but a number of Suffolk residents heeded the call to arms and journeyed west to enlist. Philander Cook, a Smithtown resident, joined the Union forces. Four regiments of New York volunteers, raised in Brooklyn, were sent south, first to guard Washington, D.C., and, later, to fight the Battle of Bull Run.

By August of 1862, President Lincoln realized, along with the rest of the

E. H. Smith made "a patriotic appeal to the young and old to come forward to rescue country and flag." Although elected as Democratic congressman, Edward Henry Smith supported the Republican president's call to arms. It is recorded that Smith's relations with Lincoln were "very pleasant" and that the president "received him warmly" on visits to the White House. Lincoln spoke kindly of E. H. Smith and said "I like to visit with you, Mr. Smith, you ain't all the time asking for something." Steel engraving, History of Smithtown, J. Lawrence Smith, 1882

The black walnut tree still stood on the south side of Middle Country Road, across from the Hallock Inn, when this photo was taken in 1890. The Hallock Inn, although altered by additions, still remains today. Mrs. Hawks, 1890, Smithtown Historical Society

Philander Cook survived his first enlistment with the Brooklyn regiment in 1861. He enlisted twice more with different units of the Union Army, first with a Vermont regiment, then with the New Jersey Cavalry Company B. He returned home to his wife and a government pension of $12 per month that he received until his death in 1912. Philander Cook died in Hauppauge and was buried in the Presbyterian Church Cemetery. A simple stone set amid some tall cedars marks his final resting place. His Civil War musket was passed down to his great grandson, Edward Walsh. Remarkably, the gun was found still loaded with gunpowder and a ball shot in 1950. The musket of Philander Cook now resides at the Smithtown Historical Society. Collection of the author

North, that this war would not be won quickly or easily. A request came for three hundred thousand additional men and this request would reach into Suffolk and the very heart of Smithtown.

Shortly after the president's request, a meeting was called by Smithtown Supervisor Joel L. G. Smith. Town residents assembled under the great black walnut tree that stood across from the Hallock Inn on Middle Country Road. Here freshman Congressman Edward Henry Smith, elected the same year as Lincoln, was chosen as president of the meeting. The purpose of the gathering was simply to discuss Smithtown's response to Lincoln's request for troops. A resolution was moved and seconded "that the Town of Smithtown raise by tax eight thousand dollars to be expended by bounty to promote volunteering for the war," and it was unanimously carried. Judge Lawrence Smith, in the *History of Smithtown* (1882), states, "The whole amount with very few exceptions was voluntarily paid, and the quota of the town was promptly filled . . . a few recusants who had at first refused to pay were compelled to do so." It was obvious even then that the call for patriotic contributions was not always eagerly received.

Fourteen men from Smithtown are known to have enlisted in 1862, although the number may have been higher. Each man agreed to a three-year enlistment, though few thought the war would last that long. Letters were written home from those assigned to N. P. Fitzpatrick's Company 2, of the 139th New York Volunteers. Smithtown's men in arms included names like: Adriance, Atkins, Burnett, Conners, Gibson, Howell, Henniger, Ryan, Henshaw, Sewell, Waterousea, L'Hommedieu, and Smith. Patriotic envelope covers with encouraging words from General George McCellan worked their way home bringing news for waiting family members. Letter, Smithtown Historical Society

George L. Booth returned to Hauppauge and his farm, circa 1890. Smithtown Historical Society

George L. Booth died in 1919 and was buried in the Hauppauge Methodist Cemetery. His headstone proudly tells of his participation with the 127th New York Volunteers in the War Between the States. Collection of the author

There were at least two Booths associated with the Civil War. One was the infamous John Wilkes Booth, the other, less well known, was George LaFayette Booth, resident of Smithtown and Hauppauge. George L. Booth joined the 127th New York Volunteers of Suffolk, known as the Monitors. He, along with a thousand other sons of Suffolk County, was trained on Staten Island, then shipped south on flat cars from New York. After three years of enlistment less than five hundred returned to their homes able to carry on their peacetime labor.

The war continued until April 1865 when General Lee surrendered the Army of Northern Virginia. The surrender of Fort Sumter in 1865 by the Confederate Army was made to representatives of the Suffolk County Monitors. Smithtown had its share of casualties in the war. Strong Soper, a member of the 102nd New York Volunteers, died as a prisoner of war in the infamous Andersonville Confederate Prison. Walter Bishop, captured by the South, died in February 1865, shortly before the end of the war.

The war was both a profoundly personal and a major national event. Its impact reached far beyond the four years of hostilities. The Civil War was a transforming force, both destructive and creative in its effects upon the structure and social dynamics of society and the lives of ordinary people. The development of Smithtown's charitable institutions, the coming of the railroad, and the commercial development of the economy were direct results of the national struggle.

The Civil War demanded a great human cost from both the North and the South. More Americans died in the Civil War than in the combined death toll of all American wars from the Revolution through the Korean War. Wessels Payne, age twenty-one, was one of those who sacrificed his life with the 139th New York State Volunteers in October 1864. The Payne Family had already established a proud history of service. Jesse Payne had marched to Sag Harbor with the Smithtown Militia during the War of 1812. Hauppauge Methodist Cemetery, photo by the author

LONG ISLAND RAILROAD

At the time of its completion in 1872, the trestle across the Nissequogue River Valley was the largest iron structure of its kind on all of Long Island. It stood over 50 feet high and spanned a distance of 490 feet. The major iron beams were brought up the river on 50-foot scows. The scows traveled only on flood tide. Although earning good money working for the railroad, the scow owners carried the seeds of their own destruction. Soon the trains carried more passengers and more cargo. Commercial river traffic ended a few short years later. Postcard, Smithtown Historical Society

Tremendous industrial growth in the Northeast continued after the Civil War. New York City strained under the weight of a rapidly growing population. Immigrants from Europe along with African Americans from the South came to take advantage of new job opportunities in New York City. Long Island farmers benefited from the city's growth. There were hungry mouths to feed and Smithtown farmers were willing to help. The problem was how to get fresh farm produce from Smithtown onto the tables of those waiting city folk. The answer came in the form of the Long Island Railroad.

The railroad was not new to Long Island, in fact, the L.I.R.R. had been chartered in 1834, twenty-six years before the Civil War, and is the third oldest railroad in the world still in operation. The original line did not pass through Smithtown. The railroad made every attempt to avoid the north shore in favor of a less populated center of the island. The object of the original rail line was to find the cheapest and fastest route from Brooklyn to Greenport. The ultimate aim was not to serve Long Islanders, but to move passengers between New York City and Boston, Massachusetts. In 1844 the L.I.R.R. began operations with unbridled success. A trip overland between New York City and Boston that took three days was shortened to 11.5 hours with the use of the L.I.R.R. Racing along at "break neck" speed of thirty mph, carrying its precious human cargo, it was the supersonic transport of its day.

A great technical miscalculation was revealed after only four years of operation when in 1848 the unthinkable became a reality. An all-rail route along the Connecticut shoreline, thought impossible just fifteen years earlier, was now open. The "Big Apple" and "Bean Town" were now connected by one rail line. The more complicated L.I.R.R. route was severely out of date. The loss of revenue brought on the railroad's first bankruptcy in 1850.

The concept of fast, dependable, railroad transportation was, however, the wave of the future. Although the L.I.R.R. was not geared to serve the Island population, changes could be made to accommodate local towns. The transcontinental railroad had been completed in 1869. Even before its completion, reports from towns along the new railroad routes were extremely positive. The new railroad towns were booming while those towns outside the tracks were fading quickly.

If agricultural Smithtown could be linked to New York City by improved rail service the residents might benefit immensely. Smithtown was interested in the future, and the future rested with the railroad. The railroad connection would not be accomplished without a cost. The creation of the Smithtown-Port Jefferson Railroad meant the town would have to raise $50,000 in cash and additional $30,000 in bonds before the railroad would agree to enter the town. This large debt would come on the heels of the heavy financial burden left by the Civil War. It was not until 1902, over thirty years later, that railroad debt would be completely paid.

Joel L. G. Smith and Carl S. Burr, from Smithtown, were the surveyors for the proposed railroad route through the town. The Nissequogue River, until then a major source of transportation, became an obstacle. A trestle to cross the river was designed and completed. The first steam powered locomotive came to Smithtown in 1872. Coming east from Huntington, the northern spur of the L.I.R.R., the Smithtown-Port Jefferson Railroad, would continue out to the terminus in Port Jefferson. The arrival of the railroad came one year after the opening of Grand Central Station. Ulysses S. Grant was in his first term as president and the population of Smithtown in 1870 had reached 2,136.

Sadly, the railroad spelled the end for commercial use of the Nissequogue River. Soon the docks of Elias and Aaron Smith, along with those of Darling and Blydenburgh, would serve less and less business. The docks fell into disrepair, rotted, and finally disappeared along with the sloops and scows that could no longer compete with the new technology.

Methods were employed that helped move goods more rapidly. Farmers would bring their wagons laden with potatoes, cabbage, cauliflower, or crates of shellfish for a quick run to the markets of New York City. The wagons would be detached from the horses and run onto waiting flatbed railroad cars. The carts and wagons could be quickly unloaded in New York. In the evening the wagons would be returned to Smithtown loaded with horse manure, fresh from the streets of the city. The L.I.R.R. had brilliantly cornered the manure concession from the New York City sanitation commission. Mountains of "free" fertilizer came back to the fields of Smithtown. Meeting the train in the evening was not the wonderful olfactory experience that one might get nostalgic about.

The railroad station in Smithtown was constructed in a style similar to the other station houses in St. Johnland and St. James. The Victorian style station in Smithtown was replaced in the twentieth century by a more modern structure. The old station was sold and moved to Lawrence Avenue, near Miller's Pond. The classic roof line is still evident in the structure even though the station has been converted to a private residence. Ess and Ess Photo, 1910, Smithtown Historical Society

Charlotte Ganz Collection, 1960, Smithtown Historical Society

Map, Long Island Railroad, Smithtown Historical Society

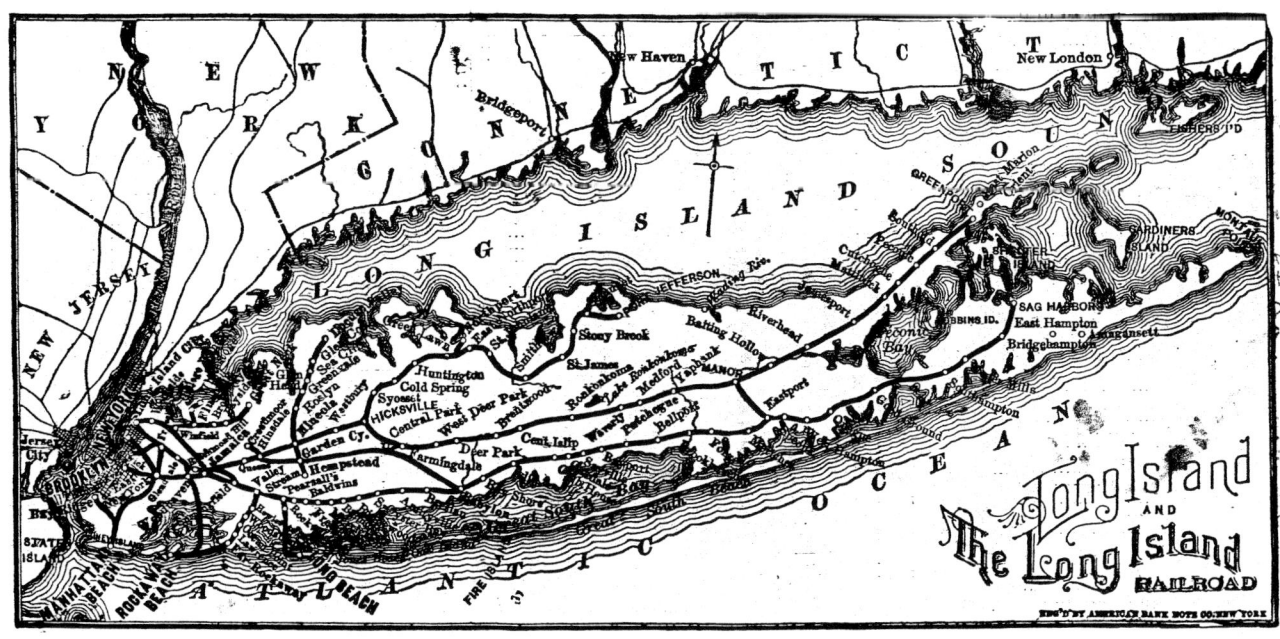

The Trainor's Hotel was built next to the Railroad Station in order to have the best chance to lure weary travelers for the night. The three-story hotel burned down at midnight on December 5, 1909, and was never rebuilt. Main Street runs to the right of the hotel looking eastward. G. B. Brainard, 1878, Society for the Preservation of Long Island Antiquities

The 1900 monthly commutation ticket for A. B. Smith allowed for the round-trip, sixty-mile ride from Smithtown to Brooklyn. The railroad manager in 1900 was, oddly enough, H. M. Smith, traffic manager for the Long Island Railroad operations. Smithtown Historical Society

Milk cans await pick up from the station platform. Poor refrigeration in 1887 eliminated the competition from the big, upstate dairy producers and gave Smithtown farmers a distinct advantage in supplying the dairy needs of New York City. The railroad attempted to increase revenue by adding Sunday "milk trains," but popular opposition quickly ended the effort to run any trains at all on Sunday. G. B. Brainard, 1878, Society for the Preservation of Long Island Antiquities

POSTAL HISTORY

Smithtown's postal history is more than two hundred years old. It began in 1795 when regular mail deliveries were dropped at the Epenetus Smith Tavern on Main Street. Benjamin Blydenburgh acted as the first postmaster in those early years. In 1819 when George S. Phillips was assigned as postmaster, the post office was moved to his home and store at the Head of the River. From the 1790s through the 1870s mail was delivered to Smithtown via stagecoach. In the mid 1870s, mail was delivered three times a day by railroad. Sacks were tossed from the speeding train as it crossed the river going east. Most of the time they landed on target. Sometimes, with a light bag or a heavy wind, a mail bag would end up floating in the river.

As the town developed, businessmen sought to move the post office closer to the commercial center. In 1889 the new postmaster, W. Benjamin Jaynes, agreed and a new post office was created on the northeast corner of Bellemeade Avenue and Main Street. The move dissatisfied patrons who lived near the old post office which had operated successfully for seventy years. A compromise was reached to create two separate post offices.

One office was centered at the Head of the River and was called Smithtown Post Office. A second, known as the Smithtown Branch, was positioned further east on Main Street. The two operated separately for the next sixty-four years.

About 1900 a building was constructed near the railroad trestle to house the Smithtown Post Office. A new post master was chosen, E. L. Arthur, who ran the General Store across the street. The 1900 post office building is occupied today by the Total Security Locksmith Shop, on the south side of Jericho Turnpike, across from "the Bull."

In the 1920s an improvement was made in postal service. Postal carriers were hired to make home deliveries twice a day. The daily ritual of picking up mail at the post office was now a thing of the past. Finally, the confusion of having a town with two postal addresses was corrected in 1953. The Smithtown office and the Branch office were combined into one simple address—Smithtown. Don't look for zip codes until the 1970s.

The Riverside Store of E. L. Arthur became the Post Office in 1890. The General Store was operated first by Mr. Smith, later by Booth and Arthur and, finally, by only E. L. Arthur. It was located at the junction of Route 25A and Jericho Turnpike. The Post Office sign is just above the front door. Caleb Smith's paint shop is at the far right. R. S. Feather, Smithtown Historical Society

The Smithtown Post Office, Head of the River, circa 1890. From left to right are: a Mr. Payne, Fred Darling, E. L. Arthur with the mail sack and Fred Booth. The Booth and Arthur Store is in the background. Smithtown Historical Society

The Smithtown Branch Post Office is the small building behind the passing automobile. The car is just passing the corner of Bellemeade Avenue going west. The corner grocery on the left has been replaced by Crest Florist. The two buildings east of the Post Office are the Royal Arcanum Hall, the unofficial town hall and polling place in 1907, and the J. S. Huntting Store. Today these two building comprise the Colonial Center Shops. R. S. Feather, 1907, Smithtown Historical Society

THE TELEPHONE

Can you imagine a world without the marvelous invention of Alexander Graham Bell? The amazing creation transmits the human voice to any conceivable distance. It would not be the emotionless sounds of dots and dashes any longer. The telegraph had coldly delivered news of births and deaths. The telephone allowed friends and family to respond easily, transmitting not only information, but the excitement and emotion of the spoken word.

In 1895 Smithtown phone service was in its infancy. The phone line out of Northport had reached Head of the River and the first phone was installed in the Booth and Arthur store. If you had to make a call or receive one, that phone was the only one in town.

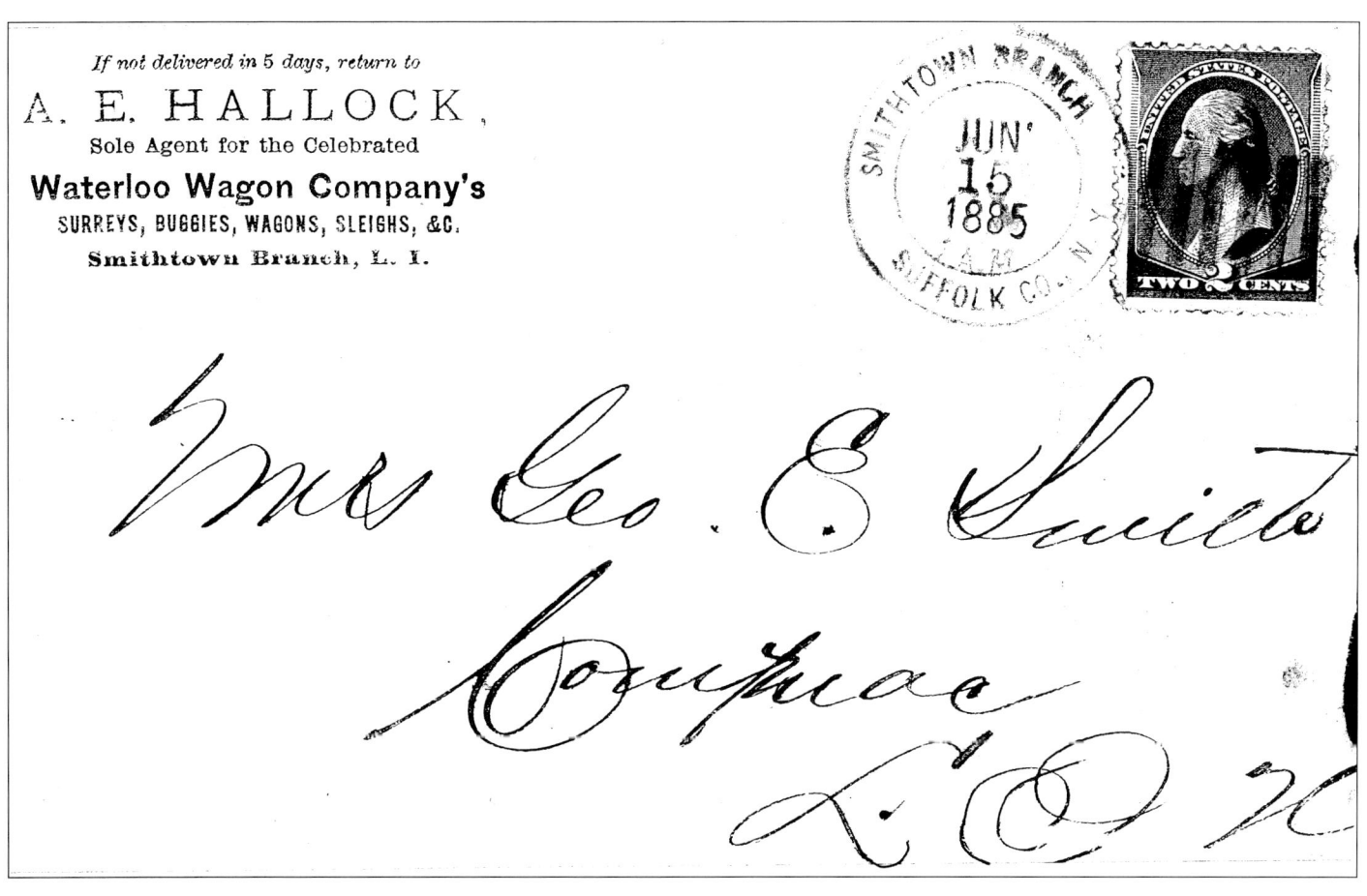

The postmark is Smithtown Branch in 1885. The Hallock Blacksmith Shop was sending correspondence to Mrs. G. E. Smith. There was no need for a street address, or zip code, or the "K" in Commac. Smithtown Historical Society

The Smithtown Railroad Station stands left of W. E. Smith's Drugstore. In 1899 Smithtown's first telephone switchboard was installed at the drugstore to service the twenty phones in town. The first telephone subscribers were local physicians, hotels and inns and, remarkably, a group of ladies that were members of the "Smithtown Recipe Club." R. S. Feather, Smithtown Historical Society

There was no dial, no touchtone, no answering machine, no call waiting, and no memory, except your own. The old oak telephone operated on two dry cell batteries, but it was still a luxury very few people in Smithtown could afford in 1900. Collection of the author

Progress was marching forward and by 1899 there were close to twenty phones in town, enough for a small switchboard to be installed in the drugstore owned by Reverend William E. Smith, pastor of the Methodist Church. The drugstore stood on the north side of Main Street near the railroad station. A local drugstore employee Mae Edwards, was asked to operate the new switchboard. At fifteen years of age, Edwards held the distinction of being the first telephone operator in Smithtown.

Mae Edwards would exchange greetings with all the customers whom she knew by name. She gave information about the weather, time, informed the subscribers about events in town and even fishing conditions on the river. The whole process was more casual than businesslike. Back in 1900 no one would dare interrupt dinner with a phone call. In fact, no one could, since the switchboard only operated between the hours of 8 A.M. and 5 P.M.

Not everyone was thrilled with the progress, as hundreds of poles carrying the phone lines marched into town. One Smithown resident, who shall remain nameless, feared that these new towering poles would attract lightning to his home. His protests fell on deaf ears, until he jumped into a newly dug post hole and refused to budge. Even the most intellectual reasoning could not move the impassioned protester. All day the man stood in the hole, unable to sit or lie down. His wife supported his effort by bringing him his lunch and dinner, as amused workers waited patiently to set the pole in place. Finally the sun set, the work crew departed, and the protester emerged from the hole, confident that he had won the contest. When he awoke the next day, the pole was set in place, accomplished in the dead of night without a sound. Progress had won out, and the telephone was in Smithtown to stay.

By 1910 the town had a hundred phones and numbers were now issued to subscribers. The phone exchange was moved to the home of Mrs. John Wood, located on Maple Avenue. By 1929 the Smithtown central phone office had grown to five hundred phone customers, and a new office was built on the west side of Maple Avenue, almost directly across from where the phone company is today.

"I'm Not A Mov'n," original drawing, Mr. Joseph Albert

THE FIRE DEPARTMENT

The development of a community is not a quick process. The establishment of a town, however, is easy. There is early settlement, followed by the arrival of new residents, and the construction of homes, businesses, churches, and schools soon follow. Roads are built as needed and government begins as the growing need demands. This is a town, not a community.

A community is a feeling, a sense of pride, not only in your own home and possessions, but a pride in the town where you live. It develops out of a loyalty to your fellow townsfolk and common trials and tribulations; collective concerns about the success of your schools and businesses. Community is a spirit, a sense of oneness that makes people feel that they are not alone, that there are people like themselves working out their lives.

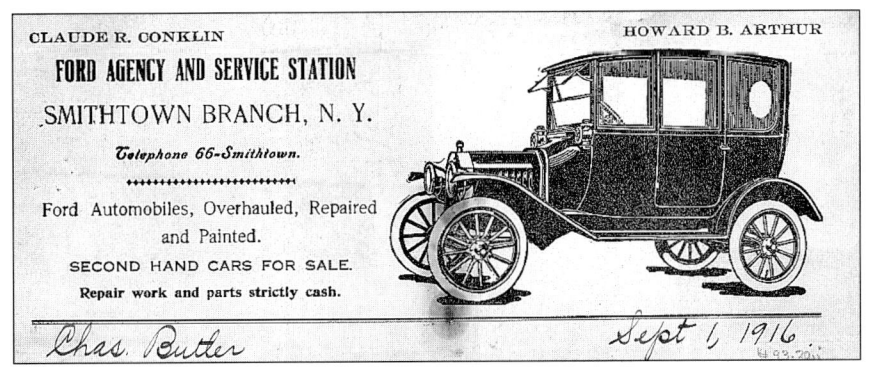

Claude Rowland Conklin and Howard B. Arthur erected a building on Main Street in 1916, just west of Maple Avenue. There several workers unloaded the unassembled Model T Fords from the Long Island Railroad freight cars. The cars were assembled and sent to Arthur Hubbs Ford dealership. In September 1916 the Ford Agency could be reached by phone, the number in Smithtown, was 66. Document, Smithtown Historical Society

The alarm tower is visible on the top left of this photo. The Long Island Railroad donated an engine driving wheel to use as an alarm signal. The first fire alarm system was instituted: one stroke—go north, two strokes—east, three strokes—south, four strokes—west; ten strokes denoted a house fire; six strokes denoted a woods fire. Clinton Darling and the new Hook and Ladder, purchased from New Haven, Connecticut, pose in front of the firehouse. Notice the leather water buckets hanging below the wagon. R. S. Feather, postcard, Smithtown Historical Society

This is not to say that a community has consensus or a single direction or plan. A community is not all Republicans or Democrats, all Christians or Jews. Disagreement between townspeople cannot destroy community spirit when the ultimate aim is the betterment of the town.

The development of a volunteer fire department is one element in the creation of that spirit. As early as 1750, the concern for uncontrolled fires troubled the town fathers. On the first Tuesday in April 1750, Town Supervisor Solomon Smith offered a resolution that stated "no fire be set in this township in the woods, and if any fire be seen in ye woods and thought to be in this township the person who first discovers ye fire shall have the right to alarm ye whole town in order to extinguish said fire, and whoever shall neglect or refuse to go upon such a warning shall forfeit six shillings to ye use of ye poor in this town."

The arrival of the Long Island Railroad through town caused great celebration, but also grave concern. The engines of the wood burning era were primitive and often red hot cinders would fly from the stack and ignite fields and woodlands along the track. Still, the town relied upon the average citizen to respond to the crisis of a fire.

The turn of the century brought rapid and unexpected changes. The coming of kerosene lamps replaced whale oil, but soon gas lighting and then finally electricity were available in town. Wood-fired heating systems and stoves were replaced with coal burning boilers. The new boilers burned more efficiently, but at a greater intensity and with increased risk of accidental fires.

The automobile brought with it a need for fuel. Naphtha and gasoline had to be stored in town buildings along with oil and grease. The twentieth century had set the stage for change. The question remained; would the community respond to the changing times?

In 1900 there was still no formal organized means of fire protection for the town. A two-wheeled chemical fire extinguisher had been in operation since 1890 at the St. Johnland facility, but that was a limited effort. Everywhere else when an alarm was sounded people would rush with buckets, shovels, and ladders to the scene of the blaze. The old and young would form bucket brigades. Water would be passed from local ponds, streams, cisterns, or wells. If there was water available, and if the alarm was spread in time, the effort might prove effective. The process was slow and most fires resulted in the total loss of the structure.

The town had suffered a few serious fires by 1906, increasing the sense of community concern. Awareness was raised that a fire could spread to engulf the entire community because of the increasing density of town buildings. People could lose not only their homes, but churches, schools, and businesses, all in one cruel moment.

On March 8, 1908, after a number of futile attempts at formal organization, a department was organized in Smithtown. Officers were elected and thirty volunteer members enlisted. The birth of the Smithtown Volunteer Hook and Ladder Company had taken place. The first company purchase was one dozen long handled shovels. J. S. Hunting, one of the first charter members and owner of the general store on Main Street, donated a small piece of land on Bellemeade Avenue to locate the first firehouse.

The firehouse was not yet built when, on September 16, 1908, one of the most serious fires in Smithtown's history confirmed the need for organized fire protection. The Hallock Blacksmith Shop on the northeast corner of Landing Avenue and Main Street caught fire. The seventy-five-foot long, three-story wooden frame building was set ablaze by a single spark on the old cedar roof. Helped by a stiff north wind, the fire was out of control in only a few short minutes. The school bell rang on Main Street, in morbid harmony with that of the Methodist and Presbyterian church bells, to alert the town of the raging inferno. Volunteers arrived but their ladders were too short to reach the third-story roof. Two large barns belonging to C. B. Darling burned as

The Hallock Blacksmith Shop burned down in September 1908. Pictured from left to right are: 1. Alanson Sturm, 2. A. E. Hallock, 3. E. Brooks Raynor, 4. George Gentry, 5. Luke Glavey, 6. Luther B. Hallock, 7. Charles Sturm, 8. Harry Register, 9. Ellis Newton, and 10. John Brown (second Floor). Smithtown Historical Society

Two days after the fire, a hook and ladder truck was purchased from Bayport Fire Department for $175. Reaching fires on high buildings was now possible. Many fires might now be extinguished before they became destructive. R. S. Feather, 1908, Smithtown Historical Society

After the Hallock Fire. R. S. Feather, 1908, postcard, Smithtown Historical Society

flames started to spread to adjoining structures. The fire would have been worse had not a large chemical tank from the Kings Park State Hospital arrived, drawn by a team of horses. It arrived in time to save the Darling house. The fire had a unifying effect on the recently formed fire department and the town. Many residents had thought the organization an unnecessary luxury. Now almost everyone realized the need for fire protection.

In November 1908 the L.I.R.R. donated a drive-wheel rim from a locomotive engine to be used as a fire alarm. Struck by a sledge hammer, the distinct sound could be heard from a great distance. When placed atop a new steel tower, the sound would travel even further. The firehouse on Bellemeade Avenue was dedicated on March 2, 1909, and it remained the firehouse until it was replaced by a modern facility on Elm Avenue in 1955.

On December 5, 1909, Trainors Hotel caught fire. The two-story building was destroyed but the railroad station nearby and surrounding buildings were saved by the quick response of volunteers. The new department had proved its worth.

The creation of surrounding fire districts and companies followed Smithtown's lead. St. James Fire Department developed slowly and with very little equipment. Early in the morning hours of January 1, 1922, the new year was greeted with an unwelcome fire which consumed a good part of the village. Public spirited citizens sparked a new drive for more department members and better equipment. Headed by Charles S. Butler and Judge Henry Weismann, money was raised for a new pumper, a new firehouse on North Country Road, and a new charter on March 8, 1922. The new St. James chief was Mr. John O'Berry.

In Kings Park, a casual but important meeting of residents was held at William H. Clayton's livery barn in 1912. The meeting was the impetus behind the creation of the first Hook and Ladder Company in 1913. Bill Clayton, along with the Bradleys, Petersons, Patikys, Gilmers, McWilliams, Strattels, Dowlings, Gheris, and Cusicks founded the first department. The initial purchases were a four-wheel wagon and a manually operated pump, pulled to the scene of the fire by hand. The Kings Park Hook and Ladder Company was formally incorporated in 1923. The firehouse was constructed in 1925 and a separate fire district organized in 1926. Other areas added departments as development and need warranted it.

An addition to the firehouse equipment was this 1909 chemical engine seen here in the firehouse on Bellemeade Avenue. The wheels and tongue were made in the Hallock Blacksmith Shop before the fire of 1908. Notice the old pot belly stove on the right. R. S. Feather, 1909, postcard, Smithtown Historical Society

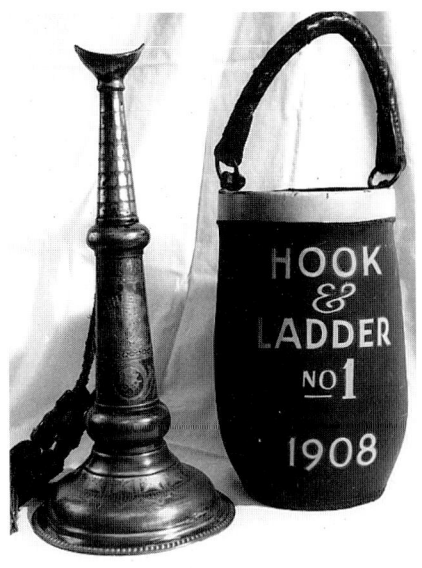

In July 1912 a silver trumpet was purchased for use by the Smithtown Chief to issue orders during fires. The old leather buckets were still part of the firefighting apparatus in 1912. Photo by the author, Smithtown Fire Department

Commack's first firehouse was built in 1908 on the north side of Jericho Turnpike where the present firehouse stands today. Smithtown Historical Society

By 1917 the firehouse had installed a new alarm bell at a cost of $94.50. The entire collection of Smithtown firefighting apparatus was proudly on display. In the first truck, a 1919 Ford, are: Driver Joseph Luisi, Chief Frank Brush, and Edward Moseley in the back. In the second truck are: Driver Earl Scott, Carlyle Hodgkinson, Charles Sturm Sr., and Freelan Jones. In the third truck, a hook and ladder, are: Driver Frank Valentine, Richard Thompson, and Howard B. Arthur. Standing by the hook and ladder is Charles W. Smith. By the firehouse door are: Joseph Hastings and two boys—Harold Purick and Theodore Brush. R. S. Feather, 1917, Smithtown Historical Society

In 1909, after the Smithtown fires and frequent losses due to fires, St. James residents met to organize the Eagle Hook and Ladder Company. On July 2, 1910, Mayor Gaynor and Congressman W. W. Cocks laid the cornerstone of the new fire house on Woodlawn Avenue. C. R. Frank, Smithtown Historical Society

The St. James Fire Company Blaze Military Band. R. S. Feather, Smithtown Historical Society

St. James second firehouse was located on North Country Road, circa 1923. Smithtown Historical Society

The Kings Park Hospital Fire Department was made up of volunteer members from the hospital staff. From left to right are: Joe DePaul (with arm over ladder, wearing hat), Jim Moten (white sweater) was head of recreation, Fred Gallery (dark suit, fedora, sits on ladder), Irving Fleischer (glasses, on running board), and Dick Gilmer (on running board) worked in the maintenance department at Kings Park and was also a local committeeman in Kings Park. Patients of Building C peer out barred windows as Peter Hildebrand, hospital photographer, arranged this classic photo. P. Hildebrand Sr., Smithtown Historical Society

From 1913 to 1926, Kings Park had hand pumpers pulled by a jitney bus. This was the first fire truck purchased by the Kings Park Hook and Ladder Company, an American LaFrance Triple Combination Pumper acquired in May 1926. It could pump four hundred gallons per minute and carried a forty-gallon soda-acid extinguisher. The cost was astronomical—$8325. Modern fire equipment would be ever more expensive. Smithtown Historical Society

The breeding and racing of horses was part of life in Smithtown. Weekends were spent at the Commack track of David Bryant or at Benjamin Newton's Driving Park in St. James. A mile track was laid out between Fifty Acre Road and Edgewood Avenue, as seen in this painting by Edward Lange. Private collection

CHAPTER 6

Hooves, Wheels, and Automobiles

HOOVES

If the sound of race horses gets your blood flowing and heart pounding, then the story of the race horse, Lady Suffolk, will just make your day. The filly from Smithtown was foaled in the spring of 1833 on the farm of Leonard W. Lawrence, located near Aaron's Landing on the west side of the Nissequogue River. The horse was sold first to Charles Little, then to Richard Blydenburgh, who thought that the gangly, large hoofed horse was better suited for pulling a butcher's wagon than for running races.

It was David Bryant who first realized the horse's racing potential and purchased her for $112.50. Lady Suffolk raced for the first time in 1838, winning a purse of eleven dollars. Both Bryant and Lady Suffolk were set on a course that kept them racing for the next sixteen years. Even though Bryant was not an accomplished horseman, he raced the horse both in harness and under saddle. Bryant was not particular about the track, its conditions, or the distance, if there was a purse to be won.

"Lady Suffolk" by N. Currier, Smithtown Historical Society

Arthur B. Lawrence is seen leaning into a turn at Newton's Driving Park in St. James. Although the horse tracks and racing parks are gone, the raising and showing of horses is still an ongoing activity in Smithtown. Haas Photo, Smithtown Historical Society

Riding was not only for men. Josephine Smith is seen taking the hurdles on the Fifty Acre Road Park around the turn of the century. Smithtown Historical Society

Dr. John Brower Browning proudly displays his horse Pong in front of the Hallock Inn during the summer of 1896. The noise of gasoline fired engines soon replaced the gentle sound of horses' hooves on Main Street. Smithtown Historical Society

In 1845, at the ripe old age of twelve, Lady Suffolk trotted a mile course in under two minutes and thirty seconds. It was the first time any horse had recorded such a feat. A few years earlier, she had run the mile under saddle in 2:26 $^1/_2$ and was attracting national attention. Lady Suffolk became a celebrated horse. People flocked to see her race against the best horse flesh in the country from Boston to New Orleans. The renowned graphic artist Nathaniel Currier, and later the team of Currier and (Joseph) Ives, immortalized her in numerous lithographs. Pictures of Smithtown's classic horse hung in barns, blacksmith's shops, and stables.

As Lady Suffolk aged, her gray coat turned white. Although well past her prime, thousands of people still gathered wherever she raced. The old girl, at the age of twenty, was still winning purses, with the equally aging David Bryant still driving. Sadly, the song about Suffolk Lady was becoming true, "the old grey mare ain't what she used to be."

While in New Orleans for a series of races, David Bryant became ill and died. The horse and owner were shipped back to Long Island to Bryant's widow. The fastest and most famous horse in racing history died a year later at age twenty-one. She had won an amazing $35,000 during her career. Unfortunately, Bryant had been too busy racing his famous filly to allow her time to continue the Smithtown blood line. The great Lady Suffolk died in 1854 without giving birth to a single foal.

There were other horse related activities in Smithtown that did not involve racing. Legend says that the English tradition of fox hunting was introduced by none other than Richard Smith, himself, back in the seventeenth century. The Smithtown Hunt was formally organized in 1900, with the selection of Mr. R. Lawrence as the first Master. On weekends horse and rider would run the fields of Nissequogue and Smithtown in search of their quarry. The members, in proper attire, are seen in front of Martin Taylor's house in Nissequogue.

Packs of hounds were exercised three times a week, even though the hunt was run only on weekends. So serious was the breeding of good hounds, that an effort was made to improve the local pack with infusion of a new blood line. In 1912 Mr. James Clinch Smith went to England to purchase several champion hounds. His return trip to Smithtown was booked aboard the ill fated *Titanic*. Survivors reported that Mr. Smith was last seen racing below deck to release his dogs and give them a chance to survive in the sea.

The Hunt. Cantor, photographer, Smithtown Historical Society

The Smithtown Polo Club was organized on March 29, 1911, by Lawrence S. Butler. The matches in Smithtown and on Long Island were taken seriously. The sport was raised to World Class Competition when in 1924, the Prince of Wales visited Long Island to watch Team U.S.A. challenge the National Team of Great Britain. Shown is the Smithtown Polo team in 1923. From left to right are: W. Brachtel, G. Wilson, A Marucchi, and C. Hart. Suffolk County Historical Society

On August 23, 1911, the following motion was made and carried by the Town Board: "That the riding of bicycles, tricycles or similar vehicles upon the sidewalks within the limits of the Town of Smithtown is hereby prohibited. Every person violating this ordinance shall be punished by a fine not exceeding the sum of five dollars for each offense, and in the case of non-payment, imprisonment in the county jail not exceeding one day for each dollar of such fine." Wilson Art Company, photographer; Richard H. Handley Collection, Gift of C. E. Rockwell, Smithtown Library

WHEELS

The bicycle craze of the post–Civil War period reached a fevered pitch by 1890. Americans wanted new technological toys created by industry. The horse was still fine, but the "safety bicycle" was new and different. Pedals, chains, sprockets, and Dunlop's pneumatic tires were a combination hard to resist. Bikes like the Eagle, Liberty, Spalding, Columbia, Pierce, Hartford, and the Monarch appeared on the scene in great numbers. However, road surfaces in Smithtown and most of Long Island made the travel too difficult.

Richard Handley, a millionaire from Hauppauge, was an avid sportsman and outdoor enthusiast. He was one of the first to embrace the new craze. He individually funded the building of a hard-surface bicycle path from Smithtown to his estate in 1892. By 1897 he had extended his path south to Brentwood, for a total distance of about ten miles.

Bicycle traffic became so heavy that a committee was appointed by the town to do something about the unauthorized use of sidewalks in both Smithtown and St. James. Bicycles were soon licensed by the county and the license fees were used to construct "side paths" throughout Suffolk. By 1900 one could travel north and south or east and west on a bicycle.

The Long Island Railroad scheduled special trains that would take a person, with his bike, from New York City to Suffolk for an extended weekend of cycling. Urban residents disembarked at Kings Park or Smithtown, then traveled by pedal power over the scenic rural paths, stopping for the night at a roadside inn or hotel.

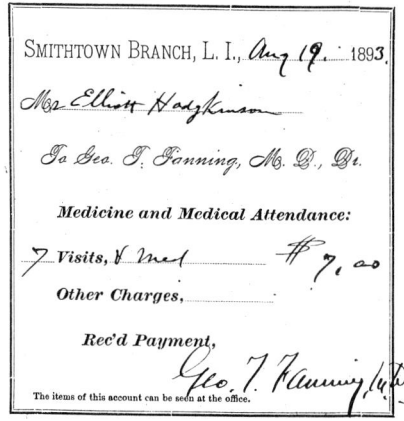

Dr. Fanning's bill. It's amazing that Dr. Fanning could afford to buy anything considering his low cost service: Seven visits, including medicine—seven dollars. Collection of Frank Stepanek

George T. Fanning was one of the most popular and well-respected doctors in town. Seated on the front porch of his home on the corner of Edgewood Avenue and Main Street, he could watch the world pedal on by. In 1890 bicycles were as popular for adults as they were for children. Dr. Fanning went on to purchase the first automobile in town. Collection of Frank Stepanek

The arrival of the first motorized means of transportation in Smithtown coincides with the arrival of Theodore Roosevelt to the presidency of the United States. The year was 1901 and the American people were watching the dawn of a new century. A physician by the name of George T. Fanning was the first to own an automobile in town. He purchased a "Locomobile Steamer," made in Bridgeport, Connecticut. In this picture, the doctor is on the left. Walter Hill Flessel, car dealer, seated next to the doctor, had just made his first car sale from his shop in Huntington. Collection of Frank Stepanek

Coe D. Smith poses with his car in 1906. Mr. Smith was known for his epic long distance drives between Smithtown and Florida in the years after 1910. The first car on the roads of Kings Park was an electric model owned by John J. Cusick. J. Evans of St. James owned a Model K Ford in 1906. In that same year, Richard Handley took his "Prescott Steamer" up Hauppauge Road to buy naphtha fuel from the J. S. Hunting Store on Main Street. John Brown installed the first gas pumps in town at his store that stood just east of New York Avenue. Virgil Merihew opened the first Chevy dealership to add some competition to Ford, on Main Street. Smithtown Historical Society

AUTOMOBILES

The turn of the century found little change in the way citizens moved about. Even after the invention of the "horseless carriage" in the 1880s, the horse remained the most common means of transportation well into the 1920s. In 1900 there were only four thousand automobiles in the entire United States. The virtual lack of paved roads in Smithtown and all of Long Island was a great hindrance to any rapid automotive development.

Probably the least known, but one of the most influential pioneers of the early automobile era was Arthur Raynor Pardington of Smithtown. He was responsible for creating the rules and regulations that governed auto racing in the early 1900s and ran the world famous Vanderbilt Cup Races, held on Long Island, for Mr. William Kissam Vanderbilt of Centerport. The great pioneer completed his career by engineering the first transcontinental highway, the Lincoln Highway (Route 30). On the day of A. R. Pardington's funeral in 1915, flags flew at half mast from New Jersey to Oakland, California, to honor a distinguished gentleman from Smithtown.

Fixing up a 1910 Buick became a project for the young men in town. The Smithtown Automobile Company operated a building behind Colonial Center Shops on Main Street. The "real" car enthusiasts, like William Leonori of Smithtown or William O'Berry of St. James, purchased the classic four-cylinder Stutz Bearcat. The purchase price of $2000, in 1913, prevented it from becoming the most popular and most affordable car of the day. Collection of Frank Stepanek

Mr. Pardington was one of the founders of the Long Island Auto Club in 1901. This classic picture of the Riverside Garage was taken in 1911. The Booth and Arthur Store is on the right, almost out of the picture. The roof on the Riverside Inn is visible behind the garage. The only building standing today is the structure to the left of the Riverside Garage, now a local tavern. This complex of buildings stood south of Jericho Turnpike across from where the statue of "the Bull" stands today. A. R. Pardington, photographer, 1911, Smithtown Historical Society

A. R. Pardington tools along the Long Island Motor Parkway in a 1904 Cross Engine Franklin air-cooled auto. A. R. is in the first car on the right. The rear automobile is a 1904 Pope and Hartford. The completed Long Island Motor Parkway stretched from Queens County to Lake Ronkonkoma in Suffolk. It was the finest private road in America, if not in the world. Collection of Frank Stepanek

In March of 1908, a committee was appointed to investigate the best material suited for construction of permanent roads. The material must have been expensive because in 1909 the town board suggested continuing "sprinkling oil" on the highways to hold down "dust" and "dirt." New road construction would depend heavily on local revenue and the monies needed would be enormous. Financing of road construction and maintenance would be an ongoing problem. A controversy about the town's costs to allow these "devil wagons" to move around town continued to take up more and more time at the town meetings.

Improved roads meant increased speed. Motor vehicle accidents became a regularity. On January 8, 1925, the town saw fit to announce a $100 reward for evidence leading to the conviction of the person responsible for the death of Carl Lorentson. He was struck and killed at Head of the River hill on December 23, 1924, at 6 P.M.

On March 11, 1910, A. R. Pardington petitioned the Town Board to allow the Long Island Motor Parkway to cross into Smithtown from Huntington. Between 1908 and 1914, "A.R." supervised the entire parkway construction shown here in 1911. The parkway was an engineering marvel. It was the first roadway to be constructed with reinforced concrete, the first ever to have banked curves for high speed driving, the first to employ a non-skid surface and safety guard rails. The roadway was built with overpasses and underpasses to eliminate dangerous intersections and it was landscaped to make it a "park" way to please the eye of motorists. Collection of Frank Stepanek

Charles P. Soper (driving) and Conrad Hansen would need quality roads. This International Harvester High Wheeler was loaded with a delivery from Soper Bottle works in St. James. Smithtown Historical Society

The effect of the automobile on Smithtown was not all joy and nostalgia. The auto, while providing reliable transportation, did present some unique problems. The old horse never produced a great amount of noise. On August 26, 1914, the town board saw fit to pass an ordinance restricting open mufflers on cars operating in the town. In June 1915 a two-by-three-foot sign was placed at the intersection of Moriches and River Road. The sign simply stated, 'WARNING DANGEROUS FOR AUTO TRAFFIC.' Even today, River Road can still be a driving adventure. On September 22, 1916, Supervisor Edward H. L. Smith advised the constable to arrest anyone operating a motor vehicle without lights at night. In 1918 the enforcement of vehicle speed laws required the town to hire Mr. Harry Smith of Brooklyn, the first motorcycle constable in town. He was paid $5.00 per day plus $1.00 extra per day for wear and tear on his motorcycle.

One of the best automotive stories involves William H. Arns who had spent much of his life in Hauppauge. His chosen trade was the repair of bicycles and automobiles. The Ford Motor Agency, owned by Kenneth Hubbs and located on Main Street, gave Bill his first job. However, he dreamed of the day when he could buy a garage of his own. His dream came true when he purchased two acres of land on the east side of Hauppauge Road (Route 111), where he began his own successful business.

One day in 1917, while Arns was at home for lunch, a man came to the door and asked if there was a mechanic that worked at the garage. Bill returned to his garage and "effected repairs" on a troubled magneto. The repairs were only temporary because the driver informed Bill that the car was

The Town was required to improve road surfaces to meet the ever increasing demands of the automobile. By the 1920s the Smithtown Highway Department was engaged in that effort. Mel Brush on the tractor along with Frank Valentine, standing, supervise the building of Terry Road. Bill Owens is on the second tractor. R. S. Feather, collection of the Valentine Family

144 E. G. Booth had moved his lumber business from Head of the River to Landing Avenue. He could now make deliveries of lumber supplies in his Model T Ford truck. The Booth Lumber Company has been replaced by the Smithtown Bowling Lanes of today. Collection of Arthur D. Phillips, gift to the Smithtown Historical Society

bound for Camp Upton, an army training camp in Brookhaven. Bill suggested that a permanent repair might be made at the army facility. The driver turned and opened the rear door of the car. Stepping out into the afternoon sun was none other than Theodore Roosevelt, the hero of San Juan Hill, the Trust Buster, and the ex-president of the United States. Arns was caught by surprise as the president inquired as to the cost of the repair. Bill apologized for not effecting a permanent repair and politely refused any compensation, "not even one red cent." The president removed his hat, shook Bill's hand with infectious vigor, offered Bill a cigar, and then introduced Mrs. Roosevelt, who was seated in the car. The Nobel Peace Prize Winner and Oyster Bay resident then entered his car for the remainder of his journey. The switchboard "buzzed" for days with news of the new friend Bill Arns had met in Smithtown.

Frank Valentine stands in front of Smithtown's first coal/wood fired "oiler." Bill Owen operated the controls. The fresh oil was covered with gravel or ash. The wonderful smell of a fresh oiled road is lost to today's youth as are the oily footprints tracked across the living room floor. Collection of the Valentine Family, gift to the Smithtown Historical Society

The improvement of Landing Avenue was done with the new, powerful tractor. As strange as it looks today, Frank Valentine called it "the first real piece of machinery that the Highway Department ever owned." Collection of the Valentine Family, gift to Smithtown Historical Society)

This accident at the intersection of Lake Avenue and Fourth Street in St. James was surveyed by the Town Constable William Howell. Stop signs and traffic lights were destined for almost every dangerous intersection in the town. Long Island Lighting Company installed streetlights at railroad crossings and heavily used intersections to improve night driving. Police photo, 1929, Ace Photo Laboratory, St. James, Smithtown Historical Society

Mrs. Samuel O. Smith and Eva Hawkins, along with an unknown small boy, pose for the photographer, circa 1890. The wagon ruts are visible in River Road on the left. The age of automobiles and wider black top roads were still a few years away. Smithtown Historical Society

CHAPTER 7

Friends and Neighbors

The township of Smithtown contains not one, but several villages, hamlets, and communities. The governmental hub has always been the town of Smithtown. Like spokes on a wheel, the hamlets of Kings Park, St. James, and Nesconset radiate from the center. The Villages of the Branch, Nissequogue, and Head of the Harbor are distinguished by their local governmental control. Other areas of Fort Salonga, Commack, Lake Ronkonkoma, and Hauppauge share their history with Smithtown and surrounding townships. Smaller areas like San Remo have created separate civic associations to address issues close to their community.

All of this may seem confusing with such an overlap of governmental authority, school districts, fire districts and even zip codes. None the less, these villages, hamlets, and communities are linked by their partnership to the town of Smithtown. Regardless of apparent separation, they all share a long, rich history

NISSEQUOGUE, HEAD OF THE HARBOR, ST. JAMES

Nestled in the northeast corner of the township are three closely related areas. The villages of the Nissequogue, Head of the Harbor, and the hamlet of St. James share not only geographic borders, but also some of the earliest history in the town.

It is near the cool water of the Nissequogue River that Richard Smith found the peace and security that eluded him earlier in his life. It was in Nissequogue that the Smith family, and succeeding generations, lived and prospered. Some of the most historic and elegant homes in the region trace their history to the founding family. Homes like that of Jonathan Smith, Job Smith, Ebenezer Smith, and Caleb Tangier Smith still stand. Over three hundred years after Richard Smith divided the Nissequogue lands "for ye use and improvement of my six sons and their heirs forever," Richard Smith IX, descendant of the patentee, still resides there.

The history of the area known as Head of the Harbor begins with deeds left by Richard Smith in 1677. In a deed "given to Samuel and Adam Smith each of them 100 acres of land in Stony Brooke neck," and again in November 1682 Richard deeded "the meadow at the three sisters harbor I

115

Timothy Mills built on land purchased from Adam Smith in 1693. The house, partially destroyed by fire, was rebuilt in 1838 by William Wickham Mills, a supervisor of the town from 1838 until 1841. Today, the large Greek revival mansion, known as Mills Pond House, is owned by the town and houses the Smithtown Arts Council. Sherwood Strong, photographer, Smithtown Historical Society

On April 24, 1732, land along North Country Road was surveyed by George Townsend for the Smith Family. Twelve fifty-acre lots were drawn and deeded to members of the Smith Family. Lot No. 8 went to Joseph Smith, son of Job Smith, and grandson of the patentee. The lot was transferred and sold, finding its way to Timothy Smith in 1839. The Timothy House can still be found on the north side of Route 25A, east of the St. Philip and James Roman Catholic Church. Collection of Mrs. Harry Van Liew

order and give my son Adam and his heirs." It was Adam Smith who built the first house on the east side of Stony Brook Harbor. Formerly, it had been named *Three Sisters Harbor*. The name, of Indian origin, referred to the three sister crops of corn, beans, and squash that the Native Americans grew upon the land.

The area grew slowly. Only a few homes had been constructed by 1850 and they centered around North Country Road and the south end of Moriches Road. It was not until 1856 that part of Head of the Harbor separated and gained a saintly designation. Smithtown Episcopalians had been worshipping for many years at the Caroline Church in Setauket or St. Marks Church in Islip town. These trips, for members traveling from Smithtown, required not only a deep religious commitment, but fortitude and physical endurance as well. The journey, by horse-drawn carriage or sleigh in all sorts of weather, was earthly penance for any family.

Other homes were built in the area. In 1845 Joel L. G. Smith constructed a large Victorian mansion known as Deepwells. At the turn of the century, Supreme Court Justice William Gaynor purchased the estate. Elected mayor of New York City in 1910, he routinely brought visitors, reporters, and government officials to his country home. Gaynor was not much different from Theodore Roosevelt. Both men were progressive reformers of the period, both were from New York, and both used the north shore of Long Island to retreat from the affairs of government. Today Deepwells is preserved through the efforts of the Suffolk County Historic Services. Smithtown Historical Society

117

The Ebenezer Smith General Store built in 1856 became the center of community life. It was general store, community center, place for tax collection, and the first post office in the new hamlet of St. James. The St. James General Store is now the oldest continuously operating facility of its kind in the United States. Since the General Store was many things to many people, the owner was doing two or three operations at once. Often people who came to pick up mail would not dismount to come in the store, but would wait impatiently outside, while Smith tried to help customers inside. Frustrated, Smith posted a sign outside of the store: "People on horseback must enter store for mail." To his amazement, a woman rode her horse into the store to request her mail, then rode out. Ebenezer's new mail policy needed to be reevaluated. Postcard, collection of the author

The growth of St. James and the surrounding area was accelerated with the arrival of the railroad in 1872. City dwellers, businessmen, farmers, immigrants, and tourists could now easily find St. James. The only original Victorian railroad station on Long Island can be found in St. James. Postcard, Smithtown Historical Society

The federal government under President James Buchanan created the U.S. Postal Service in 1856, almost three years after the establishment of the church. Post offices were created in small towns and villages across the country. There were already three post offices in the area, Smithtown, Smithtown Branch, and Hauppauge. A fourth post office was created just east of the Branch and it was named, by federal decree, *St. James*. The community soon took its new name to heart.

The great boom in development and the influx of new residents labeled the area south of North Country Road in St. James as "Boomertown." Small houses scattered in a systematic city block pattern emerged. Along streets like Jefferson Avenue and others south of the railroad tracks, cottage style homes were built through the 1920s.

The seemingly uncontrolled growth of St. James and the emergence of primitive urbanization caused the formal separation of both Nissequogue and Head of the Harbor from the hamlet of St. James. The village of Nissequogue incorporated in 1926, and two years later in 1928 the village of Head of the Harbor followed the same path. The passage of village zoning restrictions and two-acre building lots slowed development considerably. Restrictions on both commercial and industrial building has managed to preserve much of the nineteenth-century charm of these two villages.

Leading the organizational effort to start a new church was James Clinch. On July 7, 1853, at the schoolhouse on Three Sisters Road, the church society was organized. On a two-acre plot donated by Joel L. G. Smith, with an architectural design by Richard Upjohn, the Gothic style church was completed in 1854. The total cost was $2584.06. R. S. Feather, postcard, 1910, Smithtown Historical Society

Another shop opened just down the road from the General Store. Monahan's Blacksmith and Wheelwright Shop was the hardware store of the nineteenth century. When this photo was taken, the horse was being replaced by the car, truck, and bicycle. W. H. Monahan, "Practical" horse shoer, was becoming a thing of the past. From left to right are: Tom McCarthy, Ella Mae Monahan, Luke Glavey, and William Monahan Photo, gift of Luke Glavey, Smithtown Historical Society

Hotels sprang up all over the St. James area to accommodate the influx of visitors. The St. James Hotel was constructed on the southeast corner of the intersection of North Country Road and Moriches Road. Smithtown Historical Society

The Long Island Railroad and the House and Home Company combined to promote the attractive features of the St. James area. For less than $500, a home in the country could be yours. New developments like St. James Heights and St. James Park were started. The average city dweller could afford a summer home. Lots in St. James were offered to immigrants as they came off the boat at Ellis Island. This promotional flyer expounded on the quality of both the houses and the watermelons. Smithtown Historical Society

The Shore Inn, owned by Tony Farrell, was near the harbor and could be reached by carriage from the Railroad Station. Mainly a summer inn, it was demolished around 1917. R. S. Feather, postcard, Smithtown Historical Society.

By 1900 the population of St. James had reached four hundred. As more people came to the community, business activity shifted south from the General Store area. The old dirt road called Gallaghers Avenue was, by 1906, "the Avenue," and soon to be Lake Avenue. The house of Mr. Wells, the Long Island Railroad ticket agent, still stands. The large open area to the left of the Wells' house is now occupied by the St. James School. R. S. Feather, 1906, Richard and Cathy Caracciolo Collection

In 1905 a new hotel was erected on the corner of Lake and Railroad Avenues. Known as the Nissequogue Hotel, it was billed as having the latest conveniences, gas lighting, and indoor plumbing. People could arrive by train and stay summer or winter. The Stony Brook Harbor activities included swimming and boating in the warm months. In the fall, hunters checked in to take advantage of quail, rabbit, geese, ducks, and even the elusive white tailed deer that were hunted in the area through the 1930s. Postcard, circa 1906, collection of the author

"The times they were a changing" and the post office was already too far from business activity. The office had already moved from the St. James General Store to its own building on Moriches Road when this photo was taken. Monahan's Blacksmith Shop can be seen in the background. In 1913 the post office moved one more time to the center of St. James on Lake Avenue. Postcard, 1906, Smithtown Historical Society

"Bessie" White (Mrs. Stanford White) in regal attire, circa 1900. Smithtown Historical Society

By the 1890s the north shore of Long Island was being transformed into estates of the rich. The Gold Coast was stretching out from Manhasset eastward to St. James. Wealthy individuals converted farms into magnificent estates with beautiful and grand homes. One of the individuals to find St. James was Stanford White. A talented but turbulent architect from the firm of McKim, Mead and White, he married Bessie Smith, the daughter of the prominent Judge Lawrence Smith, in 1884.

The couple purchased the Carman Farm, renamed it Box Hill, and completely remodeled it between 1884 and 1902. Stanford White was one of the great designers of the Gold Coast period. In 1892 White designed the first Golf Club house in America, at Shinnecock Hills in Southampton. In 1902 his firm was commissioned to restore the White House for Theodore Roosevelt. At the time of his death in 1906 at age fifty-two Stanford White had helped design some of the most magnificent homes, churches, and gardens in the world. *Postcard, collection of Richard and Cathy Caracciolo*

One of the most unusual creations of Stanford White was the design of the Prescott Hall Butler windmill. According to the Scientific American *of April 7, 1894, "the windmill was the highest and strongest in the world," soaring 150 feet above the bluffs of Stony Brook Harbor. Copy, Smithtown Historical Society*

In 1892 Stanford White started the construction of a home for one of his wife's sisters. Kate Annette Smith had married Reverend J. B. Wetherell in 1879. After Mr. Wetherell's death, Kate moved back to Smithtown to be near her sister at Box Hill. Stanford White constructed a magnificent octagonal home of fieldstone and glass. One of the most beautiful country estates of the Gold Coast period, the Wetherell house still stands watching over Stony Brook Harbor. R. S. Feather, postcard, 1909, collection of the author

Stanford White was busy remodeling the homes and estates of Smithtown. He was more than willing to help his wife's sister remodel Sherreowogue. Built in 1688 by Adam Smith, it was the oldest homestead in Head of the Harbor. After it was acquired by Devereux and Ella Emmet, White transformed the home into an elegant country estate. W. C. Kimbell, photographer, Smithtown Historical Society

From the harbor or from land, the Butler Windmill was a landmark for many. Photograph, circa 1910, Smithtown Historical Society

Numerous youngsters of Smithtown and St. James tested their nerve and fear of heights by climbing the old windmill. R. S. Feather thought the view would make an extraordinary postcard in 1910. The panoramic view of Stony Brook Harbor was the best one could get without flying. R. S. Feather, postcard, collection of the author

The rush to St. James by the rich and famous did not end with Stanford White. Willie Collier, a prominent stage actor, built two homes in St. James. During the early 1900s he turned the area into an actors' colony. At any time, John, Lionel, or Ethel Barrymore might be seen on the streets of St. James. Actors of the period like LaRues, Bartons, Garrick or even the noted prize fighter "Gentleman Jim" Corbett summered at the Collier estate. Evening parties, Saturday swimming at the Bohemia Club, or Sunday baseball games were all part of life at the actors' colony. R. S. Feather, 1907, postcard, Smithtown Historical Society

Irish Catholics came to St. James first as day workers and then as residents. By 1909 the Catholic community was large enough to support the Saints Philip and James Catholic Church built on North Country Road. R. S. Feather, photo, 1909, collection of Richard and Cathy Caracciolo

As more people came to St. James, churches organized to meet their personal needs. The St. James Methodist Church was constructed in 1872. Tragically, this church burned on October 13, 1897, but was rebuilt on its original site at the intersection of Three Sisters Road and Moriches Road. Postcard, collection of the author

St. James Lutheran Church was dedicated in 1928. The church on Woodlawn Avenue has seen some alterations to the original design. Postcard, 1928, collection of Carole Nelson

Edward Lange painted over a hundred views of Long Island between 1871 and 1889. A native of Commack, this self-trained artist captured in his primitive but detailed painting style the Society of St. Johnland that Dr. Muhlenberg had created. Edward Lange, artist; photocopy, Smithtown Historical Society

From the high bluffs of St. Johnland a large "sunken meadow" stretched toward the west and to Treadwell's Neck in the distance. G. B. Brainard, photographer, Society for the Preservation of Long Island Antiquities

The Church of the Testimony of Jesus was one of the first buildings constructed at St. Johnland. It was built in 1869 with funds from Adam Norrie, a close friend of Dr. Muhlenberg. The small Episcopal chapel was the center of life at St. Johnland. The Chapel was destroyed by fire in 1916. Photo, circa 1906, Smithtown Historical Society

The vast expanse of the Kings Park Hospital complex extends north and east to the Nissequogue River and Long Island Sound. Hildebrand, photographer, 1925, Smithtown Historical Society

KINGS PARK—ST. JOHNLAND

As the nation moved into the beginning of the nineteenth century, reform campaigns of all types flourished in bewildering abundance. Societies were formed against profanity, tobacco, and even the transit of mail on Sunday.

Modern idealists dreamed anew the old Puritan vision of a perfected society, free from cruelty, war, class discrimination, and slavery. Mary Lyon pioneered women's education at Mount Holyoke College in Massachusetts in 1837. Dorothea Dix was planning new treatment for the mentally ill in 1843. Harriet Beecher Stowe, daughter of a one-time minister from Long Island was rallying the nation to the evils of slavery in 1850.

In New York City in 1859, a Philadelphia born Episcopal priest named William Augustus Muhlenberg founded St. Luke's Hospital to deal primarily with helping the handicapped and underprivileged. After the Civil War, Dr. Muhlenberg was concerned with the ever-declining urban scene and the terrible conditions endured by the homeless and destitute in New York City.

Although not a wealthy man, Dr. Muhlenberg envisioned an orphanage for both young girls and boys, a home for the disabled, mentally infirm, and

A view of St. Johnland in 1878 shows the facility when only nine years old. The Testimony of Jesus Chapel with its familiar steeple can be seen on the left. G. B. Brainard, photographer, Society for the Preservation of Long Island Antiquities

127

The many operations at the hospital complex were self-supporting. A sawmill cut lumber, not only for the hospital construction, but also for sale to outside customers as well. Supervisory staff worked along with the patients. Hildebrand, photographer, 1917, Smithtown Historical Society

The Kings Park School of Nursing graduated its first class in 1898. The composition of the staff by 1900 revealed that 224 out of 454 employees were Irish immigrants; only 88 employees were native born citizens. Sixty percent of the staff were women, single, and under the age of thirty. Dr. O. M. Dewing reported that women hired to work on the men's wards had a "salutary effect" and "violence and profanity decreased." Hildebrand, photographer, 1917, Smithtown Historical Society

During World War I, President Woodrow Wilson asked all Americans to conserve food. The hospital contributed to the effort with the production of its own agricultural and meat products. The Long Island Food Reserve Battalion with flags flying clears a new field in 1917. Hildebrand, photographer, 1917, Smithtown Historical Society

At Kings Park Hospital, Building "A" was used to house hundreds of female patients. The building burned in the 1960s. R. S. Feather, 1910, Smithtown Historical Society

those unable to work. He looked to Long Island as the utopia to work out his dream. In 1816 he purchased a four-hundred-acre Smith farm in the northwest corner of the township. An additional purchase of land brought the entire acreage up to six hundred within a very few years. The Society of St. Johnland was founded.

A self-sufficient operating community was developed that included a church, cottages, a home for the crippled and elderly, and a boys' home called *Chisholm*. A large portion of the land was to be farmed to supply food. Training was started for residents in a typesetting facility that also helped to generate income for St. Johnland.

Generous gifts were made by local Gold Coast residents. Mr. and Mrs. Cornelius Vanderbilt directed the building of a house for orphan girls. The $20,000 construction cost was donated along with a $2000-a-year annual contribution for maintenance. Sunbeam Cottage was a showplace with huge windows and stained-glass designed by LaFarge of New York. Built in 1881, it was given by the Vanderbilts in memory of their oldest daughter who had died on October 31, 1904. During the years that followed additional structures were completed—Sunset House for elderly couples, the New Babies Shelter in 1904, and Muhlenberg House for women in 1906.

For a long time after the establishment of the St. Johnland charitable facility, the surrounding community shared its name. There was even a St. Johnland Post Office for a period of time. In 1872 the Board of Supervisors of Kings County observed the success of the Society of St. Johnland. They decided to follow the lead of Dr. Muhlenberg by purchasing 870 acres of land adjoining the Society parcel. Against the most strenuous objections of the Smithtown Board, construction of the Kings County Farm began.

In 1885 Kings County Farm was established with three temporary cottages to provide for the care, custody, and relief of the poor and insane. The main purpose was to relieve the overcrowding in the Kings County Asylum. The population of Kings County Farm was over 200 residents by 1887 and by 1892 there were four large buildings and thirty cottages. Roads, sewers, laundries, cafeterias, and heating and electric plants were constructed to make the facility a city within itself. In 1895 Dr. Oliver M. Dewing successfully campaigned to make it a state hospital. By 1900 the patient population was 2,697 and the staff numbered 454. The patient population was greater than the entire population of Smithtown in 1900, which was 2,513.

The Patiky family was one of the most interesting and influential in the development of Kings Park. Elias Patiky and his wife Jennie immigrated to

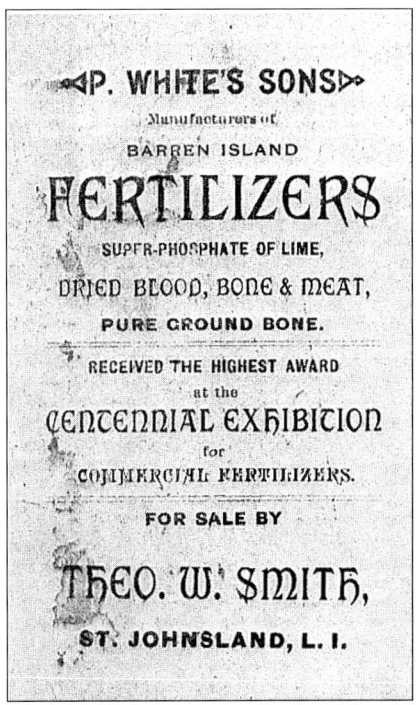

Theodore W. Smith, from St. Johnland, sold prize winning fertilizer in 1876. Smithtown Historical Society

Patients participated in various activities from band concerts, physical culture classes, holiday programs and informal parties as seen in this 1915 photo. Hildebrand, photographer, 1915, Smithtown Historical Society

One could expect to see baseball teams from neighboring hospitals, and towns at Tiffany Field, Kings Park Hospital. Collection of Tim and Peggy Dempsey

It would not be unexpected to see a Scots-Irish soccer team organized in Kings Park between 1925 and 1929. The hospital drew a majority of its labor force from Irish immigration. Baseball was an American invention while soccer was a European import. Circa 1925, Kings Park Heritage Museum

America from present-day Poland in the 1890s to escape Russian persecution of the Jews. In 1897 the family settled in Kings Park. Shortly thereafter, the Statue of Liberty in New York welcomed Gershon and Ruth Patiky, parents of Elias. The entire Patiky family, along with Uncle Sam, was reunited in Kings Park. Soon the family was taking an active role in the development of their adopted town and country. They worked with others to improve public water and to bring electricity to the town. Elias Patiky was one of the first directors of the Kings Park National Bank and the Fire Department.

Gershon Patiky had a dream greater than water or electricity. Each day as he drove his delivery wagon, he dreamed of creating a Jewish brotherhood and building a synagogue. It was the desire for religious

The Kings Park State Hospital Baseball Club of 1913 at the Tiffany Baseball Field on the hospital grounds. The manager, Tom Ash, is in the suit and tie. Ash was the manager of the Employees Clubhouse and Commissary. Dr. Macy, the hospital superintendent assigned his son as the team bat boy. Young Malcolm Macy is in the front row. Kings Park Heritage Museum.

The Long Island Railroad arrived in St. Johnland in 1872. By the 1890s the Kings Park Hospital dominated the majority of the community's activities. In 1891 the railroad changed the name of the station from St. Johnland to Kings Park. The community has been known as such for over a hundred years. T. J. McCarthy, postcard, Smithtown Historical Society

Indian Head Road looking north to Route 25A (Main Street) in 1910. George Cusick's Brooklyn Hotel is on the left. On the right, nearest the tracks, is George L. Thompson's Store, then Walsh's Saloon, and Gus Kohr's store. R. S. Feather, Kings Park Heritage Museum

In 1892 George Henry Cusick, an Irish Catholic, moved to Kings Park. He built the Brooklyn Hotel at the corner of Main Street and Indian Head Road. The hotel could hold twenty guests, even with the Cusick Family settled on the second floor. In 1916 the hotel was the first building to be electrified in Kings Park. At that time only five telephones were in town, all on the same "party line." If you wanted to get the hotel, you had to use the hotel code, "five long rings." Today the Brooklyn Hotel houses a Chinese Restaurant. Smithtown Historical Society

Elias Patiky lost his dry goods store and home. Dr. Hilander, a local dentist, lost his office and supplies when his second floor office in the C. E. Lagora Shop burned. In all, eight major buildings and a significant section of the Kings Park business district were destroyed with a total loss of more than $100,000. In 1917 that was a major loss of property for any town. Original photo owned by Ken Pross, copy, Smithtown Historical Society

St. Joseph's Catholic Church was dedicated on October 8, 1899, as Catholic immigrants produced the demand for a local parish. T. J. McCarthy, postcard, Smithtown Historical Society

freedom that had driven his family to America's shores. Gershon tried to do his best in those early years. Anyone needing the comfort and support of a traditional Jewish atmosphere could find it at the home of Gershon Patiky.

For many years it was known that a minyan could be arranged at his home even on short notice. Keeping a kosher house in the 1890s required an enormous sacrifice of time, effort and money. Weekly trips were made to New York City to purchase kosher food. Gershon and Elias tried to help other immigrant Jews get established in America. With the help of English philanthropist Baron de Hirsch, a large land purchase was made in Kings Park. The "Jewish Agricultural and Industrial Society" was created in the early 1900s to help educate individuals in agricultural techniques and skills. The project never caught on with arriving immigrants and was soon abandoned.

In 1906 Gershon Patiky's dream of a permanent center for Judaism was realized. Ten families banded together to organize a congregation. A charter was granted to the Jewish Brotherhood of Kings Park. The first president was Elias Patiky and the first secretary was Jacob Okst. The congregation bought a small house on Patiky Street. Later land was acquired for a Jewish cemetery. By 1908 a modest synagogue had emerged. Jennie Patiky organized and served as the first president of the Hebrew Ladies Auxiliary in 1911.

The synagogue on Patiky Street was only the third created in all of Suffolk County. Temple Adas Israel was built in Sag Harbor in 1899 and a second synagogue in East Setauket was constructed in 1900. The Kings Park Center was the first in western Suffolk. For more than fifty years, the synagogue served the spiritual needs of the Jewish community. Tragically, the synagogue was lost to a fire in 1962. A meaningful, dynamic spirit had been born. Gershon Patiky's dream could not be destroyed by fire. The Kings Park Jewish Center was rebuilt and the dream lives on.

Outside of the development of St. Johnland and Kings County Farm, no other single event shaped Kings Park's development more than the "Flats Fire." Kings Park had been hit by the excitement over the declaration of war on Germany on April 2, 1917. The whole country was in a state of mobilization for the war against the Kaiser. However, on May 15, 1917, a battle raged in Kings Park that forever changed the course of its development. It did not have the magnitude of the great Chicago fire, but the impact was no less significant upon its citizens.

How the fire started is not known, although it's quite definite that it was not Mrs. O'Leary's cow. Some suggest that it was open trash burning behind the Okst building; others say the origin was the billiard room or Manley Vita's Barber Shop. Whatever the cause, the wind on that spring day helped kindle a fire that still burns in the memory of old timers and their children. The fire started on the south side of Main Street in the Kings Park business area known as "the flats." The area today is located south of the commuter parking lot and eastward toward the Boulevard entrance to the hospital grounds. At 3 P.M. the fire jumped Broadway to the north side, assisted by a strong, steady breeze. Children ran from the Kings Park School to the scene of towering smoke, fire, and chaos. Dozens of men worked feverishly to move wagons and horses from Main Street. Delivery wagons loaded with everything of value were being driven or pushed ahead of the blaze. A small hand pumper from the Kings Park Fire Department arrived and started pumping water from cisterns located at Cusick's Livery Barn. The state hospital sent a fire vehicle, while surrounding communities of Huntington, Smithtown, Northport, and East Northport mobilized additional support. Smithtown's timely arrival, with a chemical engine, helped save John Cusick's building from being a total loss.

The first Protestant Church in the village was the Lucien Memorial Methodist Church. In 1892 the church was constructed on what is now the eastern boundary of Sunken Meadow State Park, facing Route 25A. In 1900 the church was moved on wooden skids through the snow to a new parcel of land at the corner of Old Dock Road and Main Street (Route 25A).

The Kings Park Fire of 1917 moved the center of the business district further west. In 1924 the new Kings Park National Bank opened at No. 1 East Main Street. The original bank directors read like the "Who's Who" of Kings Park: George L. Thompson, W. Ward Smith, Elias Patiky, E. T. Smith, H. W. Arthur, H. W. Miller, and William Reisert. Smithtown Historical Society

The original name of Route 111 was Old Hauppauge Road. This photo shows Hauppauge Road looking south from Smithtown. The stream on the right passes just south of the Waldbaum's shopping center. The wagon and rider have detoured to allow the horse a needed drink before moving on to Smithtown. Smithtown Historical Society

In 1931, almost at the close of Prohibition, an illegal whiskey still blew up in the root cellar and the Wheeler House was destroyed. The site is now occupied by a Texaco gas station. Smithtown Historical Society

HAUPPAUGE

The patent given to Richard Smith in 1665 by English Governor Richard Nicolls included the lands that contained the head waters of the Nissequogue River. The area was simply known as "Hauppauge," an Algonquin Indian name meaning "land of sweet water" or more correctly, "overflowed land." Both translations give only descriptive phrases for the abundant fresh water streams and ponds that existed in the area. Before many of them were drained or rerouted, places like Bow Drive Marsh, Forest Brook, Wheeler Brook, Hidden Ponds, Sanford Pond, and Stump Pond were familiar to old time Hauppauge residents.

Hauppauge, like its sister communities of Commack, Fort Salonga, and Ronkonkoma, shares its history with neighboring towns. In Hauppauge's case, the area is divided along Townline Road between Islip and Smithtown. The original Smithtown portion was controlled by the Smith family, first by Richard, then his wife Sarah, their sons and, finally given through a legal division of the land in 1735 to Daniel Smith II, grandson of Richard.

The Smiths who owned the land were not the first to settle it. Thomas Wheeler was the first Hauppauge resident. Sometime before 1740, Thomas built a small frame house at the present-day intersection of Route 111 (Old Wheeler Road) and Town Line Road (New Highway—1789). The Wheeler family followed a path similar to that of seventeenth-century Richard Smith. Coming from England, the Wheelers first settled in New England, at New Haven, Connecticut. They moved to Southampton, Long Island, in the 1640s, and to East Hampton in 1686, before they settled in Hauppauge around 1740. The area, at the time of the Revolution (1776–1783), was simply known as "The Wheelers" and it continued as such until 1843 when the town name reverted back to the original: *Hauppauge*. The heart of the early settlement was near the intersection of Hauppauge Road and Townline Road; Hauppauge Road was the main link between Smithtown and Hauppauge. The British marched their troops there to occupy Long Island in August 1776. Theodore Roosevelt motored down the road along with prominent Hauppauge resident Richard Handley.

Other families followed the Wheelers to homesteads in Hauppauge. The Blydenburgh, Hubbs, Wood, and Smith families all called Hauppauge home. Here they engaged in farming and the cutting of cordwood. Roads were built connecting homesteads with neighboring towns and mills. Caleb (Smith) Path, (Timothy) Wheeler Road, Joshua's (Smith) Path, and (Joseph) Blydenburgh Road give silent testimony to some of the earliest residents. The first public road in the area had to be laid out by New York

The original St. Patrick's Church was remodeled and enlarged in 1874 as new church members were added. A fire on a Saturday night in 1927 burned the unoccupied church to the ground. The mysterious brush fire occurred during the height of K.K.K. activities on Long Island. *R. S. Feather, 1917, Smithtown Historical Society*

A new St. Patrick's made of fire resistant brick was constructed in 1928 on Edgewater Avenue, near the Smithtown railroad tracks. Today the church is owned by the Catholic Church of the Resurrection, Byzantine Rite. In the 1960s a much larger Catholic Church, along with school facilities and rectory, were constructed on Middle Country Road, but the parish, now in its third church facility, still retains its original name, St. Patrick. *Smithtown Historical Society*

State legislation in 1704. Kings Highway was one of the only official roads in Hauppauge for many years.

In March 1806 two major developments occurred in Hauppauge. The construction of the first school was completed along with the development of the first church. A group of Methodists organized a church society and services in private homes were conducted by circuit preachers. Joshua Smith II, a member of the Presbyterian Church in Smithtown and a Hauppauge resident, donated land for the Hauppauge Methodist Church in 1812. A small wooden structure with a bare stud interior and long slab seats was a harsh place to worship. A stove was added over fifty years later to raise the temperature of winter services above freezing. Men and women were segregated and seated on opposite sides of the church during services. In 1835 church hymns were directed by a lead singer with a tuning fork. A progressive experiment with singers accompanied by the sounds of strings and bows ended after only a few short weeks. The "devil's music" was abandoned for the more traditional singing voices. It took almost thirty years, but in 1866 the church installed a small organ and also ended the traditional segregation of men and women. A church steeple was added in 1895, although many members thought it blatant materialism.

Irish immigrants, escaping the famine and ill fortune of their homeland, journeyed to America in the 1830s. A few Irish established homes in Hauppauge along Mount Pleasant Road north of Townline Road. These immigrants came with strong bodies to bargain for a living wage, and an even stronger Catholic faith. Early services in the 1840s were conducted in the home of a Mr. Fisher. In 1845 a church was constructed on the west side of Mount Pleasant Road. The new Catholic Church was appropriately named *St. Patrick's*.

The Smith family built a home in Hauppauge not long after the Wheelers. Joshua Smith built a typical saltbox style structure sometime around 1760. Three generations of Smiths enlarged and improved the structure. The three-story building became one of the finest architectural landmarks on Long Island.

In 1790 Caleb Smith II built a home in Hauppauge in 1790 just west of the Joshua Smith homestead. The house was given by Caleb to his daughter Sarah upon her marriage to Major Ebenezer Smith (1795–1879). They had eight children and lived in Hauppauge until their deaths in 1879. The house was destroyed by fire in 1947. Today the property is the site of

Methodist Church. Postcard, 1906, collection of Bud Land

Hauppauge's first school was operated between 1806 and 1840. In 1834 records indicate that fifty-eight children, between the ages of five and sixteen years, attended the school. A total school budget of $86 paid all school expenses for that year. Postcard, Smithtown Historical Society

This 1906 postcard shows the first of three general stores built on this site and owned by Wallace Donaldson. They were located west of the intersection of Townline Road and Route 111. The first two general stores were destroyed by fire. The last store became the home of Hauppauge's first Jewish congregation, Temple Beth Chai, before the building was demolished in 1980. *Postcard, 1907, Smithtown Historical Society*

Although this aerial view was taken in 1952, it shows the Hauppauge of the past. The large open fields were owned by Peter Zorn who raised large quantities of turkeys. At that time, Mr. Zorn owned the Joshua Smith house, located in the center of the photo. The Hauppauge Village Hall which appears on the left is now the Knights of Columbus Hall. The original hall was built in 1887 to serve a temperance group known as the "Perseverance Lodge of Good Templars." The four-room Hauppauge schoolhouse built in 1911, shown in the lower right, was demolished in 1963. Today the school site is occupied by an office complex. The Joshua Smith house was demolished and the lands were subdivided for construction of Sunnydale Homes in the 1960s. *Richard Zorn photograph, reproduced by Mr. Jack Marr, Smithtown Historical Society*

the Suffolk County Center, Fourth Police Precinct and garage on the northeast corner of Veterans Highway and Old Willets Path.
Rural Hauppauge continued to develop slowly into the twentieth century.

The Hauppauge General Store, built around 1870, housed the first post office and the area's first newspaper, *The Hauppauge Courier*. In 1907 the home of Joseph Blydenburgh located on the northeast corner of Hauppauge Road (Route 111) and Townline Road, was purchased by the Brooklyn Industrial School Association. In 1908, 257 children spent all or part of their summer in Hauppauge. Following in the progressive footsteps of St. Johnland and Kings Park Hospital, the Brooklyn facility known as Locustdale operated for forty-seven years. Children from the city were moved to Hauppauge for the summer months. "Ice Cream Days" were organized by the ladies from the Smithtown Presbyterian or the Hauppauge Methodist Churches. There were outings to Lake Ronkonkoma or Short Beach. The facility operated successfully through 1950, but was abandoned after two other camps were acquired in upstate New York.

Major Ebenezer Smith, husband of Sarah Smith, posed for this tintype portrait in 1860, at the age of sixty-five. Richard H. Handley Collection, Long Island Room, Smithtown Library

Efforts to save the distinguished home of Joshua Smith failed in 1960. Photos were taken by the federal government and filed in the Library of Congress. Parts of the interior were rescued by Henry Francis duPont for the Winterthur Museum in Delaware. The wrecker's ball struck the mortal blow in 1960 to a structure that should have been saved. E. P. McFarland, photographer, H.A.B.S. Preservation of Long Island Antiquities

The Blydenburgh home, later the Locustdale Home for Children, was abandoned and demolished in the 1950s. A Robert Hall Clothing Store was built on the site, only to be replaced by a small strip mall. The Locustdale Home was located across from Hauppauge High School, on the northeast corner of Route 111 and Townline Road. Smithtown Historical Society

At the turn of the century, an astounding number of postcards were produced featuring community baseball teams. Hauppauge was a small community but it could support a summer baseball team. Postcard, circa 1910, collection of Bud Land

COMMACK

Commack occupies the area in the southwest corner of the township. It's an area that was known as Winnecomac by the Indians who lived there. Winnecomac is an Algonquin word meaning "pleasant land." The name was later shortened to *Comac*, pronounced "Com-mac," not Co-Mack with a long O as is so often heard today.

Overlapping boundaries and conflicting claims explain why Commack was involved in disputes between Huntington and Smithtown for years. Boundaries mentioned in early deeds were ambiguous and too general, leaving many people to misinterpret their land holdings. Literacy was uncommon for both Native Americans and the colonists. Land was granted to Jonas Woods, William Rogers, and Thomas Wilkes of Huntington on July 30, 1656, by the Sachem Asharoken of the Matinecock Indians. However, in 1650 the same land had been deeded by Wyandanch, sachem of the Montauks, to Lion Gardiner and then transferred to Richard Smith. Other Indian deeds, dating back to 1646, indicated that the same land or part of it had been deeded to Governor Eaton of Connecticut.

Confusion persisted until 1674–1675, when Richard Smith successfully won his claims in both the Dutch and English courts. The boundary line was drawn between Huntington and Smithtown, with the area of Commack divided between the two. The families of Brush, Harned, Burr, Wicks, and Whitman found their families divided as well. Brothers, sisters, and parents might be found in separate townships. The dividing line between the towns became the center of community life. "Commack Corners" emerged at the intersection of Jericho Turnpike and Townline Road. Schools, churches, and stores were separated only politically. People of Commack moved freely between the two townships without much concern. Students in Smithtown might attend class on the Huntington side, while Huntington residents might cross the line to attend church services in Smithtown.

Caleb Smith II moved from Hauppauge to Commack and constructed this house in 1819 on the north side of Jericho Turnpike, near what is today the Mayfair housing development. The small building on the left was the servants' quarters. The main house was saved from demolition through the generosity of Anna Blydenburgh. In 1955 the house was moved to the Village Green in Smithtown, where it is the headquarters of the Smithtown Historical Society. E. P. McFarland, photographer, Library of Congress, copy, Smithtown Historical Society

There are fifteen members of the Whitman Family buried in the Commack Cemetery adjoining the Methodist Church. This modest church edifice is the oldest Methodist facility on Long Island, and practically in its original form. A. Biren, photographer, postcard, Smithtown Historical Society

The Civil War was ten years away when these six gentlemen sat for a photograph at the general store. This 1850 tintype captures some of Commack's early families. Seated, from left to right, are: Will Cunningham, John Hubbs, Ansell Brush, Zebulon Whitman, Tom Smith, and William Spurge. Tintype, circa 1850, photocopy, Smithtown Historical Society

The Blizzard of '88 (March 11–13, 1888) buried Long Island in almost thirty-six inches of snow. The General Store, owned by Burtis S. Harned, was often Commack's central meeting place to discuss the storm and wait for the spring thaw. Smithtown Historical Society

The Whitmans of Commack were the ancestors of Walt Whitman of Huntington. This great poet of democracy shared his time between Smithtown and Huntington. Walt was born in Huntington and taught school in Smithtown. He roamed the entire island, from Brooklyn to Montauk Point. His sympathies were clear when he wrote:

I never had happier jaunts, going over to the south shore, to Babylon, across to Smithtown and Commack and back home. The experience of these jaunts, the dear old fashioned farmers and their wives, the stops by the hayfield, the hospitality, nice dinners, occasional evenings, the girls, the rides through the brush come up in my memory to this day.

The Burr family immigrated from England in 1630. The early settlements of this prominent Commack family showed. wandering similar to that of Richard Smith. The Burrs first settled in Hartford, Connecticut, then traveled to Hempstead, Long Island in 1656. They finally settled in Commack in the 1660s. The Burr family was an important and prosperous part of the community. Their family cemetery can still be found on property which is now occupied by Models and Home Depot on Jericho Turnpike.

Commack General Store and Post Office postcard. Circa 1910, collection of Mr. Joel Streich

Commack Corners—looking west across Townline Road into Huntington township. The General Store, also known as Whitman's Store, is on the right. Postcard, circa 1910, collection of Mr. Joel Streich

The Wicks Farm House was built in 1770 on land from the original Winnecomac Patent. The house has seen vast alterations in the last 225 years. Today, the Hoyt Farm is operated as a park facility as well as a conservation and community center for the people of Smithtown. Smithtown Historical Society

Progress burst on the "Commac" scene with the construction of the Long Island Motor Parkway in 1911. Notice the guard rails that were installed along the roadway. This unique safety addition was copied by road engineers and designers all over the world. Postcard, collection of Mr. Joel Streich

In 1910 Edwin Chase Hoyt purchased the Wicks Farm. Between 1912 and the mid-1920s Hoyt developed one of the most successful orchards anywhere on Long Island. More than twenty thousand fruit trees, mainly apple and peach, supplied fresh produce to local merchants all over Long Island. Hoyt Family photograph, Smithtown Historical Society

Probably, most important in Commack history was its identification with the raising and training of horses. The Burr race track off Burr Road was one of the best known race tracks of the nineteenth century. Probably the best of all horses, Lady Suffolk, owned by David Bryant who was a neighbor of the Burr family, trotted the roads of Commack.

Another early family in Commack was that of Elnathan Wicks who secured a patent interest in 1703. His descendant, John Wicks, built a house on 350 acres in 1770. The original home, although greatly expanded over the last two hundred years, still stands along New Highway.

A note on the reverse side of this photo states, "Carl S. Burr Jr., myself drinking from the well on Jericho Turnpike." Carl Jr. joined his father in the very profitable training school for trotting horses, and constructed Suffolk's first and only one-mile trotting track. Carl S. Burr Jr., photographer, Smithtown Historical Society

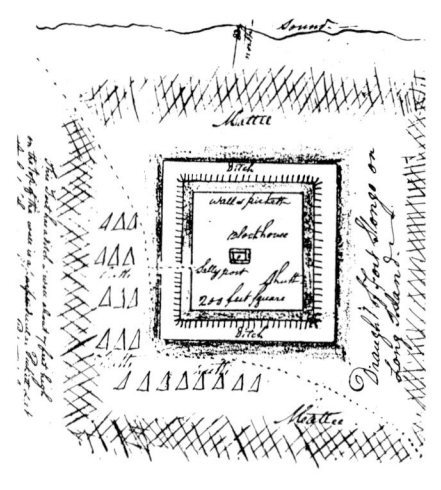

A copy of a map drawn by a local patriot was given to Lt. Henry Scudder who relayed it to Colonel Benjamin Tallmadge in Connecticut. The attack of one hundred patriot soldiers was successful. Twenty-one British officers and men were captured, four British soldiers were killed, the fort and its supplies were burned. No Americans were lost in the engagement. The original map is in the Library of Congress in Washington, D.C. Map, Library of Congress, copy, Smithtown Historical Society

FORT SALONGA

On March 24, 1695, Sarah Smith, wife of Richard Smith, deeded to her son, Daniel Smith:

100 acres at the westward bounds of Nissequogue or Smithtown as it expressed in our Patent, at a place called Bread and Cheese Hollow, and ye Fresh Pond called Unshemonuck, together with ye swamp and meadow near the pond, to be taken up in about the said hollow and pond where it may be most suitable for him.

The area spoken of in this deed is Fresh Pond, today known as Fort Salonga. Located on the northwest border of Smithtown, Fort Salonga shares its history with the Town of Huntington.

Fresh Pond is historically significant because of the Long Island Brick Company that was established there in 1684. The natural clay deposits in the soil probably provided the local Indians with the materials from which to make their pottery. The discovery of those deposits by early colonists meant a means of making a livelihood. For over two hundred years, the bricks from Fresh Pond were shipped to towns on Long Island and in New England. The Provost Brothers operated the brick yards successfully for years.

In the late 1690s reports spread that Captain William Kidd's ship, the *Adventure Galley* was seen anchored off Tredwell's Neck. On several old maps, one can find a spot marked "Kidd's Money Hole." Rumors still exist that part of a pirate's treasure may be buried somewhere on the beach at Fort Salonga.

During the American Revolution, the British constructed a fortification at Tredwell's Neck, named Fort Slongo. It was the easternmost fort along the north shore and gave a commanding view of Long Island Sound, over a hundred square miles. The fort was the site of the attack by patriot forces on October 3, 1781. The account of that battle is discussed elsewhere, but there is an interesting footnote. Sergeant Elijah Churchill was a Connecticut resident who participated in the assault on Fort Slongo. Churchill was wounded in the assault. Because of his exceptional valor, he became the first enlisted man in the American Army to be given an award. Previously, only officers were presented decorations, gifts, swords, or commendations. George Washington himself publicly commended Sergeant Churchill for his "singularly meritorious action" and went on to say, "the road to glory in a patriot army and a free country is thus open to all." Sergeant Churchill was awarded a heart-shaped piece of purple felt with the word *merit* embroidered across the face. The patch was to be sewn to his jacket as a symbol of his gallantry. The design of that first award was the forerunner of the Purple Heart medal awarded to members of the armed forces today. Amazingly, this honor had its origin at Fort Slongo in the town of Smithtown.

The close of the war found the descendants of the patentee in possession of nearly the entire Fort Slongo area. Cordwood, agriculture, and the brickyards continued to be the sources of livelihood for decades. Maps from the 1800s referred to the area as *Middleville, Meadow Glenn,* or *Tredwell's Neck*. The name *Fort Salonga* appeared when the post office was established at the Old Country Store. How the name was changed from *Fort Slongo* to *Salonga* is known only to the U.S. Postal Service. After the post office was abandoned and the mail sent to Northport, the name *Fort Salonga* remained.

The spelling of Fort Salonga was already official when this postcard was published around 1906. Baseball rivalries between villages, hamlets, and towns were strong in this period. Good ball players were actively recruited for summer leagues with promises of jobs and lodging. Postcard, circa 1906, collection of Frank Stepanek

The Country Life Store on Townline Road and North Country Road (25A) was the center of Fort Salonga activity for many years. The area is photographed from the Huntington side looking east to Smithtown. Today this intersection is made up of two banks, a gas station, and a large Waldbaums Shopping Center complex. Collection of Tim and Peggy Dempsey

LAKE RONKONKOMA

The patent given to Richard Smith included land from the head waters of the Nissequogue River eastward "to a certain fresh water pond called Raconkamuck." Lake Ronkonkoma is the largest fresh water lake on Long Island. Created by a retreating glacier, this kettle lake is located almost geographically in the center of the island.

The name *Ronkonkoma* is of Indian origin; the Algonquin word has been loosely translated as "Heading Waters," "Wild Goose Resting Place" or more correctly, "The Boundary Fishing Place." The lake was shared by four Native American bands, the Nissequogues, the Setaukets, the Secatogues, and the Unkechaugs. All of these Indians roamed the Ronkonkoma shoreline. It does not seem strange that the lake would end up controlled by three different townships—Islip, Brookhaven and Smithtown. The different Indian tribes conveyed separate deeds to the lake that were ultimately reflected in separate English town patents.

Many myths and legends surround Lake Ronkonkoma. Stories have been repeatedly but falsely told that the lake is bottomless. Other tales, from the Colonial period, tell of secret underwater connections between the lake and Long Island Sound or even Great South Bay. Indian legend claimed that the lake was enchanted by an Indian princess. She ended her life by throwing herself into the lake after her lover failed to return to her.
The natives claimed that the princess still haunted the lake and would take the life of one male every year thereafter. The large lake, with cold springs has, unfortunately, been faithful to the old legend.

Early records are incomplete, but what seems clear is that the Smithtown side of the lake was occupied by Colonial settlers by the 1740s. Captain E. Smith sold property to Thomas Biggs in 1734, "lying on the north side of Rongconcoma Pond not coming within four rods of ye said pond." By 1795 maps indicated five houses on the north side of the lake, but none to the south.

It was not until the late 1890s that Lake Ronkonkoma gained attention. Boardinghouses and hotels were constructed to accommodate an ever increasing number of visitors. Extravagant claims were made about Lake Ronkonkoma and its curative powers. Miraculous deliverance from asthma, bronchitis, malaria, digestive and nervous disorders, rheumatism and even paralysis were claimed by visitors to the lake. The railroad had little impact on the Lake development in 1844, but by 1900 the railroad helped "city folk" find the sleepy little farming community and transform it into a fashionable resort.

Local residents were not in awe of the lake, but they did realize the commercial possibilities. By the early 1920s, the lake had become a resort for anyone within a sixty mile radius. The car had made any distance reasonable, and by 1920, almost anyone could own a car.

Summertime meant boating and swimming. By the time that this postcard was printed in 1910, people from everywhere wanted to bathe in the "healing waters" of Lake Ronkonkoma. R. S. Feather, circa 1910, postcard, collection of the author

During the winter months ice skating and ice boat racing were great sport. The Lake Ronkonkoma Ice Boat and Yacht Club was chartered in 1923, and still holds races today. Classic ice boats like the Cold Wave, built to run the Hudson River, now sail the frozen water of Lake Ronkonkoma with Island "scooters" built more than a hundred years ago. R. S. Feather, postcard, Lake Ronkonkoma Historical Society

By the 1920s a series of beaches were in the ownership of local residents. There was money to be made and pavilions were constructed—Rugens, Green, Hollywood, and Raynor's became popular with visitors now coming by train or car. Arthur Turner opened a carnival-like beach front on the Smithtown side of the lake. Popular during the 1920s, the woods near Turner's Park was a good place to get "Needle Beer." It was so named because it would leave you with "tingling" or "numb" fingers. Some people actually thought that this was the sign of a good home brew during the Prohibition period.

William Meritt Hallock was not just taking his family for a ride on the frozen lake. During the winter months, individuals like Hallock cut large blocks of ice from the frozen lake. The sleds, full of hay or straw, were carefully loaded and the ice was transferred to a large storage house near the lake. Unpacked and well insulated, the icehouse protected and preserved the blocks of frozen lake water into summer. The ice was delivered to hotels, boarding houses, and even private homes. Everyone had an icebox and everyone knew the local ice man who made his regular rounds. The icebox kept food cool, not cold, and could slow the spoilage of foods during the heat of August. I was often reminded by my mother that when I said icebox I meant refrigerator. There is a difference. Postcard, Lake Ronkonkoma Historical Society

Richard Smythe sold property around Spectacle Pond with the provision that half of the pond be set aside for a public watering place, and that a road to the pond always be kept open. Spectacle Ponds are just northwest of Lake Ronkonkoma. The name, Spectacle Pond, comes from the fact that on a map the two small ponds, connected by a thin stream, resemble a pair of reading spectacles. R. S. Feather, Lake Ronkonkoma Historical Society

Turners Corner Park was located just west of the Bavarian Inn today. The rides and attractions are gone and the area is now part of Smithtown Public Beach.
R. S. Feather, postcard, Lake Ronkonkoma Historical Society

Mayor William Gaynor (with the white beard) from St. James, is on the platform to the right. The Postal Office Commemorative on February 12, 1912, captures a good representation of the entire population of Nesconset at the time, fifty residents. R. S. Feather, postcard, collection of Carl Wampole

The winter of 1916 saw Frank and his brother Nick Valentine making the mail run. Around this time Nick took over the job from his older brother. Frank Valentine went on to work for the Highway Department and later became Smithtown's Highway Supervisor. R. S. Feather, collection of the Valentine family

In 1926 Walter S. Commerdinger Jr. became Nesconset's second post master. This 1929 photo shows that he also ran the General Store, Real Estate, and Insurance businesses to keep himself busy. The building was destroyed by fire in the late 1970s. A. Biren, photographer, collection of the author

Lorentson and Son were the "power" well diggers in Nesconset. The scene, circa 1910, is along Smithtown Boulevard, near the old New York State Armory Building. Long before the arrival of the Suffolk County Water Authority, or "city water," every home and business had either a hand or machine driven well. R. S. Feather, 1910, collection of the Valentine family

NESCONSET

One of the newest additions to the Smithtown neighborhood is the hamlet of Nesconset. The area was not settled by any large number of residents until the early 1900s. The name given to the hamlet is the proper name of the sachem who headed the Nissequogue Indian band.

The difficulty for any homesteader in the Nesconset area was not only building a home, but clearing the dense woodlands that covered the area. Even in 1900, only three roads transversed the region—Lake Avenue, Gibbs Pond Road, and Browns Road. The Vion family, who arrived in 1900, almost single handedly cut the path of Midwood Avenue to access their property. Many people at that time preferred the developed communities to the north and west, so settlement in Nesconset was slow to take hold. Paul and Nicolas Spofera, immigrants from central Sicily, became the second family on Midwood Avenue. There they built a home for their five children.

February 12, 1910, was the celebration of Abraham Lincoln's birthday. The new post office was dedicated in Nesconset and Mayor Gaynor of St. James was there to officiate. There are some who believe that the name *Nesconset* was suggested by the Mayor and agreed to by the U.S. Postal Authority. Henry B. Whitaker, pastor of the Lake Ronkonkoma Episcopal Church, was chosen as first post master of the new office. Besides these two duties, Mr. Whitaker also ran the Nesconset General Store.

Louis and Antoinette Valentine purchased ten acres of land between Midwood Avenue and Nicolls Road. There they raised five sons along with some pigs, chickens, cows, and assorted vegetables. In 1912 son Frank secured a contract with the postal service to carry mail between Smithtown and Nesconset. For the sum of $35 a month, through summer heat and winter snow, the trip was made twice a day, six days a week. During the winter of 1918, the snow was so deep that horses could not manage the trip. Nick Valentine, who had taken over for his brother, walked the route carrying the mail both ways. Often in winter he would stop at Spahr's Bakery in Smithtown to pick up bread for families in Nesconset. During the spring of 1918, Nick fell victim to the influenza epidemic and died. The job of mail carrier now fell to the next son Jimmy who continued in the job for the next few years.

Charles Nicosia and Louis Vion formed a partnership and opened a small concrete block factory. Nesconset had slow commercial progress in those early years. Yet, unique pyramidical shaped blocks made by this company appeared in many local construction projects, including the original Nesconset School. Later, Mr. and Mrs. Kutil opened a pearl button factory on Gibbs Pond Road. By 1920 building had increased in Nesconset and a lumber yard opened on Jericho Turnpike east of Lake Avenue.

Bertha Friede's Lodge was in operation on the east side of the intersection of Brown's Road and Jericho Turnpike around 1921. R. S. Feather, 1924, postcard, collection of Erhardt Olsen

Bertha Friede was the wife of Anthony "Tony" Friede. Anthony's brother Frank Friede acquired the Riverside Inn in Smithtown in 1918 and operated it until his death in 1954. R. S. Feather, 1922, postcard, collection of Erhardt Olsen

SAN REMO

The large tract of land on the west side of the Nissequogue River was controlled by the Smith family from the seventeenth century. When the final boundary disputes with Huntington were settled, deeds were handed to Philetus Smith, great grandson of the patentee.

In 1793 a dock was constructed near the mouth of the river by Adam Darling, William Blydenburg, and Mills Phillips. The land was owned by Aaron Smith, and so the name of the new dock became *Aaron's Landing*. Schooners loaded with cordwood left Aaron's Landing bound for New York City and ports in New England. Those same schooners returned with cargo for Smithtown.

New docks were constructed in 1796 by Hamilton Darling and in 1800 by Elias Smith. In 1821 Elias Smith built a house on a small hill at the end of Landing Road. He gave the home to his daughter Phebe Tredwell Smith and her husband Leonard W. Lawrence. It was on this property in 1833 that the famous mare Lady Suffolk was foaled.

A landmark of San Remo is the Obadiah Smith House. Built sometime around 1700 by the grandson of the patentee, it represents one of the finest of early eighteenth-century homes in Smithtown and all of Long Island. The structure, now almost three hundred years old, has been restored and preserved through the efforts of the Smithtown Historical Society which acquired ownership to the home in 1960. Circa 1880, Smithtown Historical Society

Lawrence House. Circa 1925, collection of Tim and Peggy Dempsey

A typical beach outing at Beckers Beach after Richard Handley's purchase of the Elias Smith properties. Beach wear was still formal, even in the heat of summer. Form fitting bathing suits were still twenty years away. Richard H. Handley was behind the camera when this picture was taken, circa 1900. The guests included, clockwise from the left: Ada Strong, Mary L. Handley (hat), unknown, unknown girl, Arthur Lawrence (boy), unknown woman, Julia Lawrence (in black dress), unknown woman, Charles Lawrence (the boy at the head of the table), Homer Reboul (white hair), and Mrs. Germond of Hauppauge (seated next to him). Richard Handley, photographer, Smithtown Historical Society

Iovines Bungalow. R. S. Feather, circa 1925, collection of Tim and Peggy Dempsey

The Samuel Smith House was built in the 1770s on a hill where Landing Avenue and St. Johnland Road meet. Later owned by William Henry Mills, it became a large farming homestead in the period from 1863 to 1900. In 1929 the house and property were purchased by the Franciscan Brotherhood and became part of the St. Anthony's School Complex. Smithtown Historical Society

The house passed through a few owners until it was purchased by the Greek Orthodox Church in the 1930s. The site became a summer camp and later a boarding school for underprivileged youth of Greek ancestry. A chapel was constructed in 1947 and at that time it was the only Greek Orthodox facility between Montauk Point and Hempstead in Nassau County. River traffic helped build the fortunes of those who controlled the various landing facilities. Even the general population benefited, since the town often taxed a percentage of the profit secured at the docks.

By 1900 the railroad had siphoned off much of the river trade. The lands around the river lost their commercial value. Richard H. Handley, a Hauppauge resident, purchased about two hundred acres of the area from St. Johnland Road to the Nissequogue River. The old Elias Smith dock was then known as *Handley's dock* and was located at the end of what is today Riviera Road. The dock and beach became more recreational than commercial.

In 1918 the New York State Conservation Department closed the river to the harvesting of shellfish. Pollution from the hospital outflow had damaged the river severely. The oyster and clam industry that had contributed to the local economy was gone.

In 1922 the Courriere Holding Company, which owned the Italian newspaper *Il Progresso* purchased 194 acres of land along the west side of the river. The plan was to sell subscriptions to the Brooklyn publication, along

In 1925 a group of summer residents share a lighter moment at the San Remo Clubhouse. In the photo, from left to right, are: Marino Bittoni (pointing), Anna Bittoni (with necklace), Mario Bittoni (man with young girl on shoulders), Vinnie Pucci (boy under Mario), Arnold Discorsi (black sweater), Ralph Bittoni (waving), along with a blurring Mrs. Pucci (flowered dress). Collection of Tim and Peggy Dempsey

with the opportunity to purchase a small, twenty-by-one-hundred-foot lot in Smithtown. Generoso Pope, president of the roaring '20s money-making operation, named the new community after the Italian Riviera, *San Remo*. The main road passing through the new community was aptly named *Riviera Drive*.

Italian city dwellers, escaping the summer heat of New York City and Brooklyn, journeyed to San Remo. Without zoning restrictions, small cottages and even tent dwellings were erected. Parcels of inexpensive land sold quickly. Tomatoes were planted along with eggplant and cucumbers, as the San Remo soil produced an even greater harvest of American dreams. By 1932 when Smithtown adopted its first zoning map, San Remo had a population density greater than any other part of Smithtown. Community activities centered around the vast number of Italian residents. A clubhouse was constructed for the residents by the Courriere Company on Bales Drive.

Anyone who remembers San Remo in the 1920s remembers Jim Ferraro's Grocery. Originally open only in the summer, it soon became a full-time operation. Customers would arrive, greeted by chickens roaming in and out of the store. Children took advantage of Mr. Ferraro's dock. A rope hung over the dock allowed swimmers to swing into the river. Careful attention had to be paid to the tide, or an enthusiastic youth would find himself stuck in the soft muddy river bottom.

Swimming activities at Ferraro's dock would be interrupted every twenty minutes with an announcement from Mr. Ferraro, "Lemon ice, fresh lemon ice only 5 cents, the bigger the boy, the bigger the cup." Everyone knew that Ferraro made the best Italian ice east of Brooklyn and he kept right on making it through the 1950s. Collection of Tim and Peggy Dempsey

The Darling-Brush-Lackman House stood opposite the Smithtown Presbyterian Church in the present day Village of the Branch. There was nothing odd about a few sheep on the front lawn, it eliminated the need for weekend mowing. This house was replaced by the Village Diner on the southwest corner of Main Street and Route 111. I believe the diner has lamb chops on the menu, in memory of this photograph. Society for the Preservation of Long Island Antiquities

Looking west on Middle Country Road past the Homestead of Judge J. Lawrence Smith. It was Judge Smith who wrote a History of Smithtown in 1882. The impressive "ship mast locust" he planted along the roadway can still be found today. The white picket fence stretched along almost the entire north side of the road from house to house up to the Presbyterian Church. This photograph captures the very height of rush hour traffic in 1908. R. S. Feather, collection of the author

THE BRANCH

Smithtown was a very large area, and people needed to use specific names in order to distinguish one place in town from another. The main section of the Nissequogue River was known as the *Upper Landing*, or *Head of the River*. There was also a northeast branch of the Nissequogue River that crossed Hauppauge Road (Route 111), south of the town; this area was simply called the *Branch*. There were other names such as the *Landing, Bushy Neck, Darlingtown, Northside*, the *Common Crossing* and the *Going Over*. These names represented familiar characteristics that local people could easily identify.

Indoor plumbing was real progress in the Branch. These three privies (outhouses) stood behind the Darling-Brush-Lackman House at the intersection of Route 111 and Main Street, circa 1928. Smithtown Historical Society

In the early seventeenth and eighteenth centuries, the settlements of the Branch and Head of the River developed separately at opposite ends of the town. In 1872 the arrival of the railroad had a unifying effect on town development. Commercial interests boomed as new businesses, shops, and houses were built along Main Street. Soon the town was connected into one continuous link from east to west. However, people still felt comfortable referring to the eastern part of Smithtown as the *Branch*. It did not help to have two separate post offices which perpetuated the separate identities. People referred to the *Smithtown Branch Post Office*, the *Branch School*, the *Branch Hotel* and, even, the *National Bank of Smithtown Branch*.

In 1912 the creation of a Town Hall gave Smithtown a permanent seat of government. The Town Hall was constructed at almost equal distance between Head of the River and the Branch. As the town developed in the post-World War I period, debates grew over the operation and need for municipal services. The demand for disposal facilities, improved fire protection, and public water created a rift among various townspeople. Some saw merit in a municipal system of services, especially public water. Others wanted only a private company, or private wells to satisfy the town's needs. Residents argued over whether public taxes should be used to pay for these changes. Boundaries for water districts were drawn and then redrawn. There was talk of zoning regulations to come and certain landowners resented any government interference. People along Edgewood Avenue, the Landing, and the Branch closed ranks and moved to incorporate their own separate villages. Nissequogue was incorporated in 1926 and the example had been set. In 1927, in a final vote, Landing and the Branch voted to incorporate. Within a few years, the Landing disbanded, leaving only the Village of the Branch.

It began as a tiny village of less than one square mile with 162 residents, but the Village had set a course for local control and autonomy that exists some sixty years later. Village boundaries encompass some of the finest historic homes along the north side of Middle Country Road. Traveling east from the Smithtown Library, one can find the Erastus Arthur House, the Franklin O. Arthur House, the Hunting House, and the Hallock Inn, all dating from before the Revolutionary War. The Homestead, at 205 Middle Country Road, may date from as early as 1690, while the old Methodist Parsonage and Presbyterian Manse date from the 1830s and 1840s. Other important structures like the Epenetus Smith Tavern, the Old Library, and the Brush Barn have been moved to the Historic District created by the Village of the Branch in the 1960s, which is now on the National Register of Historic Places.

The National Bank of Smithtown Branch was chartered in 1910. The building still stands on the north side of Main Street, west of the Presbyterian Church. Sandwiched between other buildings, the old bank now houses the Smithtown Chiropractic Associates and an optometrist, Dr. Keith Dworkin. R. S. Feather, 1910, Smithtown Historical Society

No longer the National Bank of Smithtown Branch, the new bank was simply the Bank of Smithtown when it was constructed in 1924. The bank stands today with two large wing additions to the east and west. Tomlin postcard, Smithtown Historical Society

The home just east of the Smithtown Library on Middle Country Road was built in 1830 by Mr. White, who was a tailor in the Branch. The home was soon known as the Tailor-White House. It was later sold to Augustus Silliman who converted it into a bakery. In 1910 the bakery was purchased by Henry Spahr, shown here with his family. In the front, from left to right, are: Henry Spahr, Ruth Spahr (Quarterman) in the back, William Spahr, and Ada Spahr holding William Jr. Smithtown Historical Society

The J. S. Huntting Store on the north side of Main Street, west of Bellemeade Avenue, became the Great Atlantic and Pacific Tea Company. The A&P replaced the general store concept of the 1800s. You just can't beat those A&P prices in 1924: Red Circle Coffee 25 cents, Iona Tomatoes 8 cents, or Del Monte Peaches 23 cents. From left to right are: Edward Wagner, Robert Brown, and Albert Evans. Today this building is part of the Colonial Center. R. S. Feather, 1924, postcard, Richard and Marie Sturm Collection

The Smithtown Methodist Church was constructed in the Branch on the west side of Judges Lane in 1845. The four houses seen past the church were all built between 1800 and 1825 and are standing today. The Methodist Church remained at this site for another seven years before being moved. G. B. Brainard, 1878, Society for the Preservation of Long Island Antiquities

In January 1885 the Methodist Church was transported from Judges Lane west to a new site on the south side of Main Street just east of Maple Avenue. Using teams of horses, block and tackle, and massive timber skids, the building was inched forward fifty feet at a time across the frozen ground. The entire move took six weeks and became the event of the year. In 1895 a steeple was added to the church, only to be removed in 1935. The church was demolished in June 1962 and a small grocery store, Blue Jay, took its place, and much later Strawberry Field. Smithtown Historical Society

The Methodist Church still stood near the top of Maple Avenue when this picture was taken in 1909. Looking north from Bowers Court toward Main Street, numerous homes can be seen on the west side of the road. Today, large commercial buildings at No. 70—80—98 and 100 Maple Avenue have replaced the residential dwellings. What is missing in 1909 are the large maple trees so much in evidence today. R. S. Feather, Smithtown Historical Society

The Charles Sanford House on the southwest corner of Elm Street and Main at the turn of the century. Today Chemical Bank holds dominion over the site. Smithtown Historical Society

Probably one of the great benchmark storms of the nineteenth century was the spring storm of March 13, 1888. The "Blizzard of '88" hit without warning. There were no five-day forecasts, no radio or television storm advisories. A drift of almost twenty-five feet covered sections of Main Street. Only the top of the Methodist Church near Maple Avenue is visible in the distance. The Sanford House (now Chemical Bank) is on the left. Imagine, no massive snow removal operations, and no make-up snow days for school. Smithtown Historical Society

Charles Sturm ran a harness shop located in the Hallock Blacksmith Shop on the northeast corner of Landing Avenue and Main Street. It was a popular meeting place to stop and discuss politics or the affairs of the day. The building burned in a spectacular fire in September 1908. Smithtown Historical Society

Charles Sturm was a typical hard working resident in 1906. His tax assessment showed a man who owned a house on one-quarter acre of property, and an additional building lot for which he paid a total tax of $3.10. You had to really love your dogs since their assessment raised his property taxes almost 25 percent. Owners of cats could only smile! Collection of Richard and Marie Strum

A view from the top of Golden Hill looks south toward Main Street. The magnificent home of Charles D. Miller, town supervisor (1920–23), stands west of Bellemeade Avenue. Miller started the first Boy Scout Troop in Smithtown in 1913. The Miller house stood opposite the J. S. Huntting Store and Royal Arcanum Hall. The Miller House was demolished to make way for commercial development along the south side of Main Street. Today the North Fork Bank, Old Street Pub, and Grand Union occupy this site. Photo reproduced by John F. Heslin, Smithtown Historical Society

The Central Hotel in 1910 had been George Penny's Hotel and before that the home of Elijah Brush. This was only one of the many hotels that were scattered throughout Smithtown. This building stood on the southwest corner of Lawrence Avenue and Main Street. The site today is a used car lot, just east of the Smithtown Movie Theatre. Postcard, Smithtown Historical Society

The William Call Farm stood on the north side of Main Street just west of the Bank of Smithtown. The house became the office of Dr. Frank A. McGilvery and Dr. Kulke, until development replaced the house with a commercial bank building, now occupied by Greenpoint Savings, at the corner of Bank Street. Gift of Adford C. Peirce, Smithtown Historical Society

Smithtown's first and only Town Hall was completed the same year that Woodrow Wilson won the election for the president of the United States, 1912. Up until that time town meetings were held in various buildings from the Hallock Inn to the Royal Arcanum Hall. Town records were kept in the home of whoever had been elected Town Clerk. In 1913 Town Hall received two modern improvements, electricity and a phone. Can you notice any changes in the area since 1912? Smithtown Historical Society

The Nichols Family Homestead stood on the north side of Jericho Turnpike west of Edgewood Avenue. The land was sold, the house demolished, and replaced in the 1960s by Billy Blakes Stores, then Tri-County Flea Market, then "Buy Low and Sell Low." Photo gift of Adford C. Peirce, Smithtown Historical Society

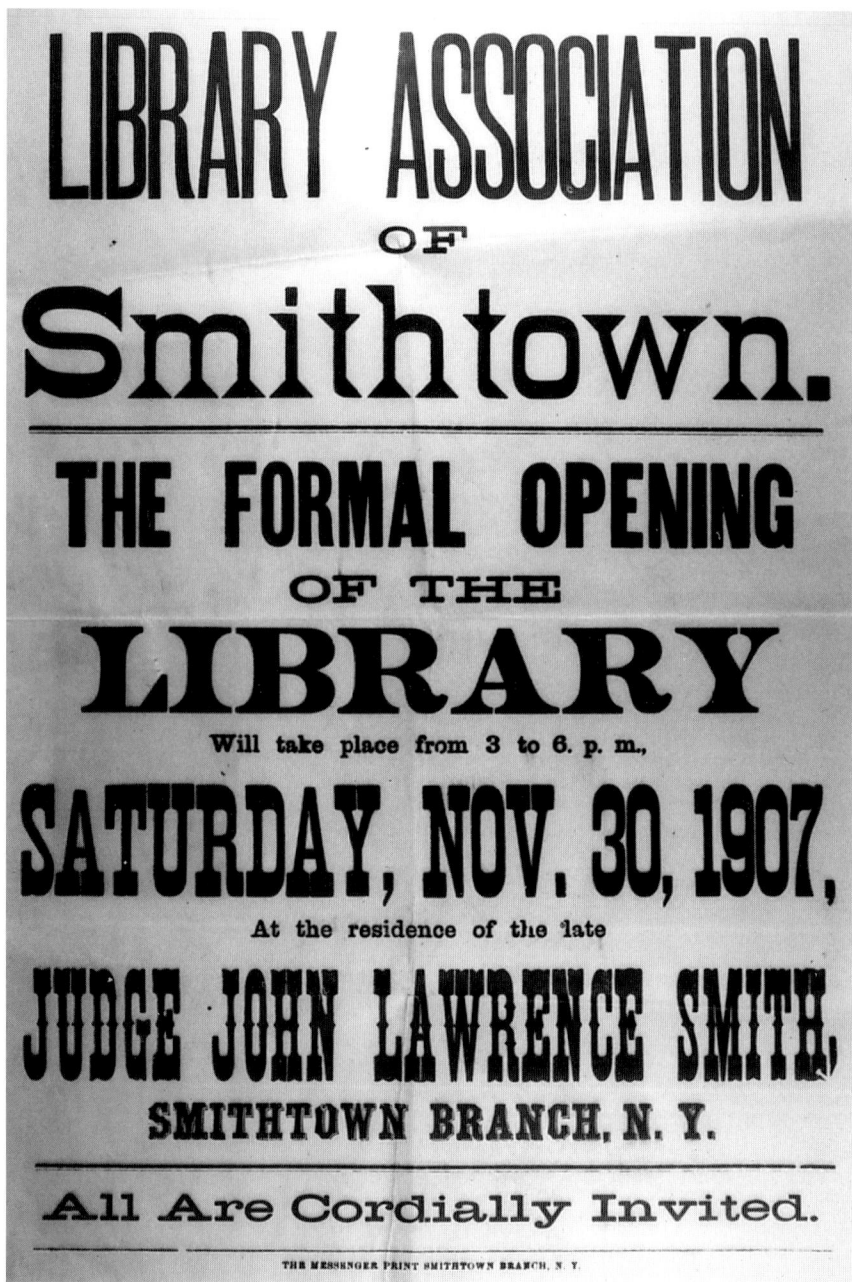

In 1907 some Smithtown residents sought to revive the idea of a library association. The growing literary crusade sparked Smithtown's second Library Association. Again, this was not a publicly funded library, but a small private association that believed a collective library system would benefit the town. Smithtown Historical Society

CHAPTER 8

The New Century—A New Age: 1900–1929

LIBRARY

The year was 1828 and shortly after the election of Andrew Jackson as president of the United States, Smithtown began to develop a library system. In December shares were sold to Smithtown residents that would make them partners in a library loan organization. This was not a public library, but one open to those who had the desire and the means to purchase membership.

The first library is believed to have been housed at the Inn of Thomas Halliock (Hallock), located on Middle Country Road, in the Village of the Branch. The inn of the nineteenth century should not be confused with a bar or tavern of today. It was a gathering place for most public activities. Room and board could be had for travelers, circuit ministers, teachers, or businessmen. Hallock Inn was a polling place and had been the setting for many town meetings. The Inn was not an improbable place for the location of a lending library association. Only five books remain of the library's original collection. One book, numbered 111, is William Prince's, *Short Treatise of Horticulture*, book two is Goldsmith's *Animated Nature*, the third Goldsmith's *Roman History*, the fourth by Reverend Michael Russell, *Palestine, the Holy Land*, number 330, and last a new edition of the *Federalist*. These books suggest two things about Smithtown's early library—a popular interest in both agriculture and politics and, second, that the library held at least 330 books. Sometime prior to 1870, the first library association fell into disuse and formal borrowing ended.

Following the Hallock experiment, a small wood-frame building was constructed almost directly at the intersection of Route 111 and Jericho Turnpike. Until the early 1900s, it was referred to as the *Reading Room*, not the library. There were books, magazines, and newspapers, but none could be borrowed or removed from the Reading Room.

The nineteenth century was drawing to a close with a dramatic improvement in learning throughout the nation. Educational facilities were

In the summer of 1909 the library was moved from the Homestead into the old Reading Room on Main Street and Route 111. Cornelia Peek was now in charge of the facility. The library had 1,602 volumes and an average of 32 books per day were borrowed between 1907 and 1909. Richard H. Handley Collection, Long Island Room, Smithtown Library

now being supported by public funds. Increasingly, adults and young alike sought ways to satisfy a thirst for knowledge in a rapidly changing world.

The purchase of books, while still expensive, was dropping in cost. The invention of linotype in 1885 and generally improved printing techniques improved book quality immensely. Books had become a major source of edification and enjoyment for the masses. The well-stocked library could be a poor man's university. The New York Public Library opened in 1895 and the Library of Congress building was opened to the public in 1897, providing thirteen acres of floor space in the largest and costliest edifice of its kind in the world.

The 1890s found Americans devouring millions of "dime novels." As literacy increased, so did America's love of reading. Even though many "paper backs" were frowned upon by parents, goggle-eyed youth read them

The second Library Association set up shop in the home of Judge Lawrence Smith, a room in "the Homestead" at 205 East Main Street. Members of the association were asked to pay five dollars a year to support the library. The privilege of borrowing books could be had by any resident merely for the price of a library card, 25 cents. Richard H. Handley Collection, Long Island Room, Smithtown Library

in hay lofts or in school rooms, carefully hidden behind the covers of a geography book.

Commack library began simply in 1915, when the Commack Neighborhood Association managed to secure a loan of twenty-five books from Albany and another hundred books from the Smithtown Library. On Tuesdays during the summer months, Miss Minnie Van Brunt, the school teacher of the Old North School, took care of the new 125-book lending library.

Other branch libraries were established slowly. In 1920 Miss Hattie Pedrick volunteered to keep a small number of books at her home in Hauppauge. She procured books for residents by carrying them back and forth on her bicycle. Miss Pedrick learned the reading patterns of her friends and kept them supplied for years. In December 1920 in St. James, Miss Ethalinda Jackson opened another branch library in the Parish House of the Episcopal Church.

Mrs. Richard H. Handley gave her husband's Long Island History collection to the Smithtown Library in 1921, as a permanent memorial to her husband. That collection is still housed in the Smithtown Library and it is one of the better collections of Long Island materials anywhere in Nassau or Suffolk Counties.

The old Reading Room was uninsulated and poorly heated. The winter of 1909 was cold and blustery so the Library Association decided to move the book collection along with Miss Peek (shown here) to the warmer confines of the Epenetus Smith Tavern until the weather warmed up. Smithtown Historical Society

By 1911 the community of Smithtown was ready to publicly support a library system. The Library Association was dissolved and its funds were transferred to the town. Mrs. Prescott Butler, a charter library association trustee, donated property for a permanent brick structure to replace the Reading Room. The cornerstone of the new library was laid in 1912. Photo, gift of Morgan Blydenburgh, Smithtown Historical Society

Looking east past the porch of the Darling-Brush-Lackman House toward the Smithtown Public Library. Today you would be looking at the intersection of Main Street and Route 111 from the steps of the Village Diner on the south side of Main Street. Society for the Preservation of Long Island Antiquities

The new Smithtown Public Library was moved north to the Village Green at 1:00 A.M. on November 15, 1950, because the building was directly in the path of the State proposed improvements to the intersection of Middle Country Road and Hauppauge Road. The original building is now a wing of the expanded facility and houses the Children's Reading Room and collections.

In 1980 the Smithtown Branch Preservation Association, with the help of the Smithtown Historical Society, rescued the Old Library Association Building. The structure was moved to Middle Country Road and restored. It now rests between the two earlier library sites, the Homestead and the Epenetus Smith Tavern. A young Noel Gish Jr. inspects the restoration efforts. Collection of the author

A temporary isolation hospital was constructed next to a house on Darling Avenue, located between Maple Avenue and Route 111. The hospital was placed near Potter's Field, because health officials thought that the death toll would be high and burials of victims should take place quickly. Luckily, the epidemic was not as severe as expected and few succumbed to the disease. The hospital was later dismantled, but the house and Potter's Field remain. Smithtown Historical Society

IF YOU HAVE YOUR HEALTH . . .

The progressive reform movement swept through Smithtown with projects like St. Johnland, the Kings County Asylum, Locustdale Home in Hauppauge, and the Howard Orphanage in Kings Park. Not all of the efforts in Smithtown were so grand in design. Some of the projects were small and aimed to benefit the local townspeople.

In April 1906 the Society for Lending Comforts to the Sick was begun in the home of Mrs. W. F. Darling. Mrs. Edward H. Tyler, Mrs. Buell Williams and Miss Helen Blydenburgh attended the first organizational meeting. The constitution said in part, "the object of this society shall be to loan any medical or surgical appliances, or any articles of comfort owned by the Society to the sick in their own homes."

The constitution further stated that anyone who contributed money or articles for the Society to use would become a member. Any person in need of articles could procure them by simply presenting the Society with an order signed by a doctor. Blank orders were given to two town doctors, Dr. Guy H. Turrell and Dr. Frederick Peterson. The first year, eighty-two items were loaned by the Society, including crutches, splints, and one No. 14A, listed as a Bombay Water Cooler, (whatever that is!). Other articles like bandages, gauze, infant's clothes, and pneumonia jackets were sold at a nominal cost. In 1906 money was raised to endow a bed at St. Luke's Hospital in New York City, which patients could occupy free of charge. Fairs, rummage sales, and cake sales along with entertainment at the Assembly Hall were held to benefit the Society's efforts.

In the early years there were no hospitals in the area and patients had to go to New York City for care. Mrs. Henry Chatfield Smith, a registered

Assembly Hall Ticket for Lending Comforts Benefit, circa 1910. Smithtown Historical Society

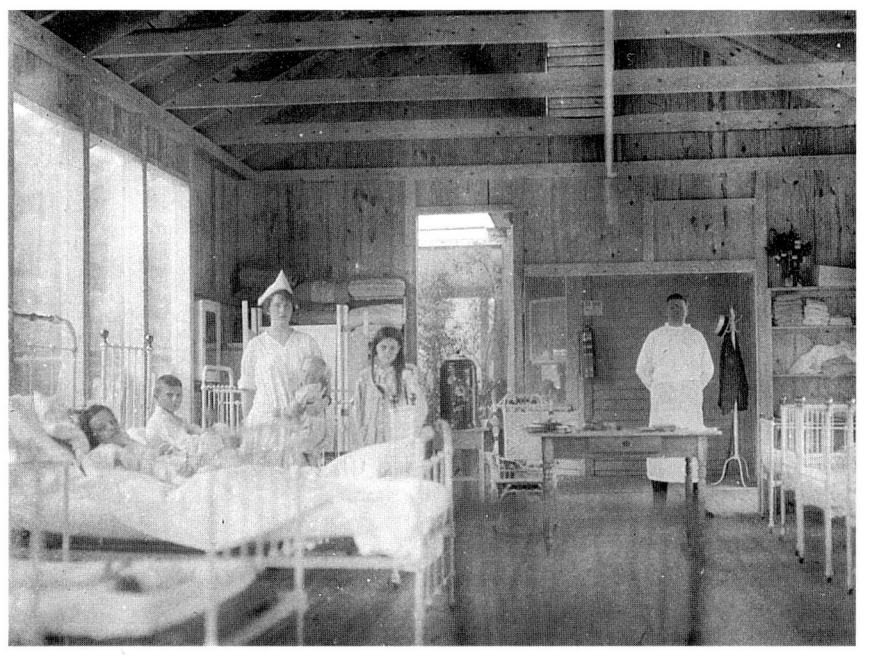

An outbreak of infantile paralysis in 1916 sent panic waves through Smithtown and neighboring communities. Parents were asked to travel without their children. People in cars were stopped and asked for identification, while roads between Lake Ronkonkoma and Smithtown were patrolled. An isolation facility was built to house children suspected of carrying the disease. Again in 1918 another nationwide epidemic struck. Influenza was the new feared disease. More Americans died of the "flu" in 1918 than had died in combat in World War I. While all Smithtown worried, only a few residents succumbed to the virus. Fate had spared the town once again. Smithtown Historical Society

nurse and Society member, accompanied the patients from Smithtown to New York on the train.

During the outbreak of infantile paralysis in 1916, a nurse was hired to care for adults and children stricken by the disease. Miss Gertrude Moffat was given the position and became the first public health nurse in the township. With no means of transportation, Miss Moffat often walked as far as Commack and St. James on her visiting duties, for which she was paid $85 per month.

The Society also started a program that gave milk to all students in the first six grades of Smithtown Branch School. Each day, in the morning, one half-pint of milk was distributed to any child needing or wanting it. The aim was simply to improve the general overall health of the youngsters attending school. The program was so successful and popular that it continued into the 1930s. At that time the State of New York saw fit to institute a free milk program in the public schools.

The Society's purpose as expressed in 1906 seems equally applicable today, "Our object is charity, in the Biblical sense of the word, offering comfort and sympathy to the sick, rich and poor, of any nationality, or religion, those of our own families and the stranger within our gates."

Patriotism was alive in Smithtown during the war years. The National Bank of Smithtown organized all five Liberty Loan Drives, starting in 1917. The small flag on the left indicates that Smithtown met its quota in the third Liberty Loan Drive. Smithtown residents collected more than $316,000, tripling the town's quota. The large flag suggests that war saving stamps were still needed to help the government's war effort. Faith Smith Collection, Smithtown Historical Society

In 1917 the call to arms by Woodrow Wilson was met with patriotic zeal. Camp Upton was created to train tens of thousands of troops in Brookhaven. Here in Smithtown the "Home Guard" took their work seriously. C. E. Rockwell Collection, Smithtown Historical Society

R. Lawrence Smith commissioned the building of two four-masted schooners that were launched in 1917, just as the war began. The two ships named Hauppauge *and* Commack *were constructed in Wilmington, North Carolina. On May 20, 1918, the 228-foot* Hauppauge *was fired upon by German submarine U-151. The U-boat captain allowed the crew to board the lifeboats before setting charges to sink the schooner. The* Hauppauge *capsized but did not sink. Righted and restored, the ship sailed until 1929 when she was abandoned on the Mystic River in Connecticut, a victim of the Depression.*

WORLD WAR I

The Great War, or the First World War, burst into flames in Europe in the summer of 1914. America was bogged down in a worrisome recession and a peace-loving Woodrow Wilson was not ready to lead the United States out of isolation. Even in 1916 incumbent Wilson won a close presidential election with the campaign slogan, "He kept us out of war," while Smithtown and the rest of New York voted for the losing Republican candidate, Charles Evans Hughes, an ex-governor of New York (1906–1910).

It was a sad President Woodrow Wilson who led America into a war against the Kaiser in 1917. Smithtown first awoke to the fact that the country was at war when the draft was announced. There would be no "purchase exemptions" and no "hired substitutes" as there had been in the Civil War. All men between the ages of eighteen and forty-five were required to register. The Town of Smithtown sent close to three hundred men into the fray. They joined an American force of almost four million men, and, for the first time, women as well. Patriotism boomed as it never had before, even greater than during Civil War or the Spanish American War of 1898. Citizens in Kings Park, St. James, Smithtown, and surrounding towns lined the streets near the train station as draftees headed off to boot camp.

A Smithtown Chapter of the Red Cross was organized on June 13, 1917, with 230 members. Chairman Morgan Blydenburgh, Vice-President Mrs. F. C. Peterson, Secretary Frank Brush, and Treasurer Wilson Ritch Jr., led the fund raising effort and managed to raise $24,453.36. Large quantities of piece work were produced by the Red Cross for the war effort. There were 12,130 hospital and refugee garments made, 91,620 surgical kits assembled, 2,925 articles knitted for the boys and three huge clothing drives for the devastated civilian population of Europe. A Smithtown Junior Red Cross and a Y.M.C.A. Association organized youth groups to help in the war effort.

Patriotic parades, circa 1917, rallied support for the "war to end all wars." The parade marches east across the railroad tracks near the Smithtown Hotel. In the 1930s an underpass was constructed to eliminate this crossing. Today the Smithtown Hotel is Angelo's Restaurant and is huddled next to the west side of the underpass, near the train station. Smithtown Historical Society

The list of men in service reads like a Who's Who of Smithtown—Vail Blydenburgh, Dr. Charles Brush, George Cusick, Harold Conklin, Cornelius Dowling, George Hallock, Guy L'Hommedieu, Edmund Smith, Robert Smith, Lawrence Smith, Harry Smith, and Frank Nicolls. Smithtown sacrificed its youth "to make the world safe for democracy." Herman Thompson, John McHugh, Allan Crowe, Fortunato Vitello, Leon Williams, Wilson Ritch, Egbert Raynor, and Donald Munro were among the fifty-three thousand Americans lost in Europe.

There are two additional family names that deserve special recognition. The Sherwood family of St. James sent four of their eleven children into active service in 1917. Joe, Edward, George, and William were brothers who had immigrated with their family to the United States in 1908. Now, less than nine years later, the brothers were sent in different directions in service of their adopted nation. Joe entered the navy, Edward was assigned to a camp in Virginia, while George and William were assigned to separate army units, the 313th and 316th Infantry Division and sent to France. In September 1918, while their units passed near the front lines in France, the two brothers met briefly, exchanged greetings and hugged before the war separated them again. Less than two months later the Sherwood family received news that William had died on October 16, 1918, and George had perished on November 8, 1918, just seventy-two hours before the armistice was signed.

The Great War ended at the eleventh hour of the eleventh day of the eleventh month of 1918. At war's end Kings Park Methodist Church decorated to welcome the "dough boys" back home. Copy, King Pedlar, Smithtown Historical Society

James Ely Miller of Smithtown volunteered for infantry duty in 1911, long before the draft call in 1917. While in the New York National Guard, James helped organize the First New York National Guard Aero Squadron. In July 1917 this aviation enthusiast was made captain of the First Reserve Aero Squadron in France. His experience and expertise made him a natural choice to organize America's first flying school and in Issoudon, France in 1918. Having established the school and trained his squadron, Captain Miller turned down a promotion to the rank of major and requested combat duty. He got his wish, but while on a mission on March 9, 1918, Miller failed to return. The following day a German aircraft flew low over a French air field and dropped Captain Miller's personal effects. James Ely Miller was dead and of all the aviation firsts, the most unique distinction was that he became the first American aviator to be killed in France in World War I.

While in Europe Captain Miller urged his military aid and chauffeur to take up flying. After his death the young army chauffeur named Eddie Rickenbacher went on to become one of the most celebrated World War I flying aces.

Today, the American Legion Post No.1152 of St. James is named in memory of the Sherwood Brothers. The Smithtown American Legion Post No. 833 is named for James E. Miller while the Kings Park Post No. 944 is proudly named for Donald C. Munro. The heroic men and women from Smithtown who served, fought, and died should not be forgotten. The stories must be preserved and retold so that future generations will not forget their sacrifice.

UNVEILING
OF THE
MILLER TABLET
AT
MILLER FIELD
STATEN ISLAND
ARMISTICE DAY, NOV. 11, 1924

Wild Ape of Smithtown and Norman O'Berry. Joseph Albert, artist

WILD APE

The Great War was being fought in Europe. American boys in the summer of 1918 were fighting in the second Battle of the Marne. Here, in Smithtown, the local men were fighting a war of their own. According to the account of Norman O' Berry and Town Board minutes, part of the summer of 1918 was spent hunting "the Wild Ape" of Smithtown. Not just a myth, a missing link, or big foot, but, according to eyewitnesses, a "great ape" loose amid the jungles of Smithtown.

This wild, hairy beast was reeking havoc on the local population. Eye witness accounts said that it could throw stones with deadly accuracy and it was reported that the creature had been responsible for the deaths of some wandering dogs. The beast had even attacked innocent women and children in the same manner. Then, amid the sounds of screaming, it would disappear into the woods again.

Men would take time to hunt the wild beast and Norman O'Berry, as a small boy, went along as often as he could. In mid-August, young Norman with his father, mother, neighbor William Smith, and Bill's sister Annie drove to Long Beach, where the creature was last seen. As O'Berry and Smith went hunting, the remaining three family members stayed in the car. All of a sudden the car started to shake. Norman turned his head and found himself nose to nose with the fearsome creature. The terrifying screams brought the return of two breathless hunters. But, the ape was no where to be found, the phantom of Smithtown had disappeared again. The car loaded with nervous passengers headed back to the safety of their homes with new stories of their dreadful encounter.

On August 18, 1918, only a few days after the incident, resident William Clark shot and killed a ninety pound wild ape in the Long Beach area. That same week on August 22, Bill Clark received, from the town, a payment of exactly $16.90 for killing the dreaded creature. How that exact figure was arrived at by Bill and the Town Board is not known. But, the threat to Smithtown had ended.

The great ape of Smithtown was more than likely a chimpanzee or a young orangutan. Rumor said that it was a fugitive from a ship docked in the vicinity of Port Jefferson harbor. King Kong it was not, but to Norman O'Berry and his family, it must have seemed like one on that August day in 1918.

WOMEN'S SUFFRAGE

The call for women's suffrage began as a declaration in Seneca Falls, New York, in 1848. The real struggle did not gather momentum until the early 1900s. The road was a hard one since many members of both sexes scorned the idea of a vote for women. Suffragettes organized and rallied across the state. The Lake Ronkonkoma Equal Rights Suffrage Club began in 1912. Prominent Smithtown suffragettes traveled to Riverhead, New York City, and Albany to gather support. Mrs. Lathrop Brown of St. James, Dorothy Miller Smith, and Mrs. Frederick Peterson were among those who advocated change. Smithtown Messenger publisher, Lawrence Deutzman, and Kings Park State Senator George L. Thompson gave their strong support for suffrage early in the struggle. Even so, in 1915 voters in New York and Smithtown rejected the vote for women 748,332 to 553,349.

Two more years of effort, parades, rallies, marches, and speeches brought a different result. On November 6, 1917, New York State male voters approved statewide Women's Suffrage by a vote of 703,129 to 600,776. The voters in Smithtown approved amending the State Constitution. The movement for Women's Suffrage that began in New York at Seneca Falls in 1848, was concluded in Smithtown almost seventy years later. Smithtown had voted to expand democracy and to increase the power of the people.

In 1918 Smithtown voters, now both men and women of the Second Assembly District, elected the first woman to the New York State Assembly—Ida Bunce Samis. It was two more years of work before women could vote on the national level, but New York and Smithtown had already led the way for change.

Rosalie Jones is seen making a point to a male voter in 1913. Yellow ribbons tied to hats or worn on lapels were the mark of solidarity for the Women's Suffrage Movement. R. S. Feather, Lake Ronkonkoma Historical Society

PROHIBITION

The great experiment of the 1920s was loudly supported in Smithtown, not only by the K.K.K., but by local churches and societies as well. Cheers rang out with the passage of the Volstead Act of 1919, that was to become the 18th Amendment to the Constitution.

The call for Prohibition had been heard early on in Smithtown. The Women's Christian Temperance Union was organized locally in the Presbyterian Church in March 1889. The first president was Mrs. William E. Smith, wife of the Methodist pastor. Various local ladies championed the reform movement, Mrs. C. Brush, Cornelia Peek, Martha Mills, Mary H. Seaman, Mrs. Paul Edwards, Emma A. Tyler, Ada F. Spahr and Blanche E. Gould.

The local W.C.T.U. was happy when prohibition of alcohol became law, but Prohibition simply didn't prohibit. "Home brew" and "bathtub gin" became popular. There were a dozen or so "speakeasies" from St. James to Kings Park where a cocktail or two might be had for the right price and the right password.

There was a great concern over this accident at the corner of Old Hauppauge Road (Singer Lane) and Main Street in 1929. A truck loaded with some "consumable prohibition stuff" was involved in a fender bender. Luckily, any potential fire hazard was removed by the quick action of local residents. First hand accounts reveal that no lives were lost and not a drop spilled. The Old Town Theater is visible in the background. Smithtown Historical Society

KU KLUX KLAN

The history of the 1920s, while fascinating to study, is also one of the most difficult periods of history to understand. The starry-eyed idealism that led America into World War I gave way to disillusionment in the years that followed. Americans feared the Bolshevik Revolution of 1917 and its importation to America. The "old stock" in America urged politicians to set up strict quotas to protect our shores from a new wave of aliens and their philosophies.

Long Island was only a reflection of America in the 1920s, no better, no worse. The response to the dramatic societal changes in America produced national stress and drove many to join the new order of the Ku Klux Klan. It is estimated that one out of every eight Long Island residents belonged to the K.K.K. Only eighteen-year-old, white Gentile males, born in the Protestant faith in the U.S. could become Knights of the Klan. Spurred on by the postwar feelings of uncertainty, membership in the clan grew on Long Island and in Smithtown.

The K.K.K. in Smithtown did not think of itself as extremist, but patriotic, not intolerant but intelligent, not for persecution but for Protestantism. It was an organization that on the surface voiced the right ideals. How could membership in an all American, Protestant, Anglo-Saxon organization that preached anti-liquor, anti-gambling, and anti-Darwin be evil? The clan only wished to return America to the days before the Great War. The twentieth century had been a period of rapid change. The clan was a reactionary force that opposed any change from traditional thinking.

Besides Klan funerals there were Klan marriages, christenings, and parades organized throughout Long Island. Smithtown Historical Society

181

The night riders of the 1870s in the South were resurrected on Long Island. People were easily drawn to the adventure, visual excitement, mass gatherings, clandestine rituals, and the thrill of secret membership. The K.K.K. had active membership among ministers, sheriffs, and town politicians. Many local candidates in the twenties actively sought K.K.K. support. Women founded auxiliary units, dressed their children in clan garb, and made the organization a family affair. On Long Island, at meetings in Smithtown and Lake Ronkonkoma, members discussed ways of keeping the Irish Catholic Governor, "Alcohol" Al Smith, out of the White House in 1928. Stories spread of Al's secret plan to make the Pope vice-president, or to secretly move the Catholic leader to Washington, D.C. Sometimes, the homes of "undesirables," most often Irish Catholics or Italians, were searched under the pretext of looking for illegal liquor. Many times this was done by civilian K.K.K. members with the approval of local authorities. Shoot-outs and high speed chases with evil rum runners were carried out to rid America of "illegal booze." All the while, the Gold Coast mansions of the north shore openly bathed in the finest liquors with almost tacit approval of the same local officials.

Many hard working, decent citizens were labeled "undesirables." The K.K.K. in Suffolk tended to be more anti-Catholic and anti-Jewish than anti-black. The black population had been decreasing in Smithtown since 1900 and the new "foreign threat" seemed to be of greater concern to many local clansman. In Hauppauge, crosses were burned on the lawn of

The Ku Klux Klan was not a secret organization in Smithtown. The white hooded members with their faces uncovered were seen burying one of their own. Proudly waving the American flag with a minister in attendance, the whole ceremony is watched by the Smithtown Constable, William Howell (with back to the camera near post on the left). Smithtown Historical Society

Wallace H. Donaldson, the local general store owner. A burning cross was set in the field across from St. Patrick's Church on Mt. Pleasant Road on at least three occasions and at the home of Reverend Father Ducey with residence on Lake Avenue. Even prominent Smithtown merchant Mr. Schechter was not immune to the intimidation imposed by the local K.K.K.

One of the Island's largest meetings was held near the Hauppauge Methodist Church in June 1923. A huge crowd of people turned out for the "Bible Thumping Jubilee." Mr. Gilbert (Gil) Hubbs of Hauppauge recalled seeing the Klan Kave (meeting) in a field now occupied by Hauppauge High School. The faithful and the curious came to the meeting from Jamacia, Queens, and Montauk Point. Under the flickering of the torch lights, Klansmen extolled the virtues of anti-liquor, pure womanhood, the Holy Bible, and a society purged of foreigners and their ideals. The headlights from automobiles around the field bathed the area in an eerie glow, as American flags waved from every bumper of every truck and car. To a small boy, the huge burning crosses, fiery speeches and cheering crowds left a powerful impression even fifty years later.

There were local residents who publicly voiced displeasure with the clan and its ideals. Muriel Spahr remembers that her father, Lawrence F. Deutzman, interrupted a local K.K.K. meeting at the Assembly Hall on Main Street. He strode into the closed meeting and told the local Smithtown members gathered that they should "be ashamed of themselves for having such a meeting, and that they "should go home to their families." Mr. Deutzman, owner and publisher of the *Smithtown Messenger*, then returned to his house on Edgewood Avenue. Later that evening, the family endured the expected—a burning cross was set on their lawn.

The great Wall Street crash of 1929 woke Smithtown out of its Roaring Twenties dream. Everyone needed all the friends they had if they were to make it through the tough times. The depression created an obligation for people to work together regardless of race, religion, or political persuasion. Confrontation and courageous opposition from numerous Smithtown residents slowly eroded away the credibility of the hooded order. The increased popularity of the American Legion, coupled with the religious harmony that was long associated with Smithtown, was too pronounced for the clan to maintain its power. The reality was that Smithtown was too diverse. Irish Catholics, Polish Jews, Russians, Germans, and African Americans were all a vital part of the community. The U.S. Supreme Court had attacked the clan, banning its secret membership and openly questioning its motives. In 1933 the government of Franklin Roosevelt ended Prohibition and robbed the clan of much of its legal clout. The Ku Klux Klan fever had run its course in Smithtown and most of Long Island. Although acts of bigotry and ugly intolerance still occurred, the officially sanctioned acts of the clan were over by the mid-1930s.

LINDBERGH

Photo of Lindbergh. Underwood, postcard, collection of the author

Daily News *Studio Photograph, Library of Congress, Long Island Forum, May 1983*

It was May 20, 1927, when a young man known as the "Lone Eagle" took off from Roosevelt Field bound for Europe. On May 21, 1927, the *New York Daily News* announced the first solo transatlantic flight. The paper also proudly displayed the only known photograph of Charles Lindbergh after takeoff. A *Daily News* photographer had followed Lindbergh in a trail plane for the first hundred miles. The picture, although labeled by the *News* as located over Lake Ronkonkoma, was taken over Hauppauge, at New Mill Pond, later known as Blydenburgh Park. Richard Brush, of Hauppauge remembered the epic event: "Oh yes, he flew Northeast over the New Mill Pond. He was low, just above the tops of the trees."

Moments later, eleven-year-old Charles Embree Rockwell was doing his morning chores before heading off to school. While on his way to feed the chickens, he heard and saw two planes flying northeast over his family farm at 245 Middle Country Road in Smithtown. He didn't know it at the time, but it was Charles Lindbergh, bound on a course that took him over Smithtown, Connecticut, Massachusetts, New Foundland, the Atlantic Ocean, and into history. It must have been an awe inspiring sight on that Friday morning. The tree where young Mr. Rockwell stood that morning was known by him and his family for years as the "Lindbergh Oak." The next day on an old static filled radio, the Rockwell family listened to the broadcast of Lucky Lindy's arrival in France. Rockwell went on to fly the oceans himself. As a pilot for United Airlines, he flew the Pacific on routes between New York and Hawaii. By that time, flying the oceans had lost its mystery and become almost commonplace. But in May of 1927, a flight across the Atlantic Ocean was anything but commonplace for a young, twenty-five-year-old airmail pilot, named Charles Lindbergh.

The home of C. E. Rockwell is part of the Village of the Branch historic district. The 1750 home was donated by Rockwell to the Town of Smithtown and now houses part of the Smithtown Historical Society's education program for young people. The sleigh in this photo is now in the collection of the Museums at Stony Brook. R. S. Feather, Smithtown Historical Society

AFTER 1929

The Smithtown story obviously does not end in here, but it is a good place to pause. Other events and issues profoundly shaped Smithtown's history in the years that followed: the Great Depression, World War II, the Cold War, Baby Boomers, Television, Rock and Roll, Civil Rights, the Feminist Movement, Vietnam and the "environment." It must be left to others to document those remaining years and their effect on our town's development.

My hope is that we can all have a part in preserving Smithtown's history for future generations. We must not forget to preserve the little things. I urge all residents, young and old, to be aware, when cleaning out Uncle Tom's trunk or Grandma's attic, of those photographs, postcards, diaries, and artifacts. Those pictures of the Boy Scouts, Girl Scouts, club meetings, church outings, winter storms, hurricanes, or interesting events need to be kept so that today's youth can "peek" into the past. It will not be long before very few will remember World War II, "school air raid drills," "hula hoops," and the "milkman." Recycle your history, pass it down, or pass it along for safe keeping. The Smithtown Historical Society has acted as a repository for important town memorabilia for over fifty years. As hard as it is to imagine, these days will be the "good old days" to those who pass this way one hundred years from now.

BIBLIOGRAPHY

Adams, James Truslow. *History of Southampton*. Hampton Press, 1917.

Albert, Gerry. "Nesconset Post Office." *Long Island Forum*, June 1977.

Bayles, Richard. "Sketches of Suffolk County." 1874

Borden, Miles. The *First 100 Years, 1892–1992*. Lucien Memorial Methodist Church, Kings Park.

Braunlein, John. *Colonial Long Island Folklife*. Museums at Stony Brook, 1976.

Brown, Mrs. Charles Hilton. *Smiths of Smithtown*, April 1927.

Cavaioli, Frank J. "The Ku Klux Klan on Long Island." *Long Island Forum*. Amityville, May 1979.

Curtis, Ann Farnum. *Three Waves, Story of Lake Ronkonkoma*. Ronkonkoma, 1976.

Deutzman, Lawrence F. *Smithtown.* /Smithtown Chamber of Commerce.

Earle, Alice Morse. *Home Life in Colonial Days*. MacMillan Company, 1898.

Ellis, David. *A Short History of New York State.* Cornell University Press, 1957.

Epenetus Smith's Tavern, Dedication Journal. Smithtown: The Smithtown Branch Preservation Association, 1972.

Fagan, Norbert. *Smithtown Hunt 1900–1964*. Smithtown.

Frankenstein, Alfred. *William Sidney Mount*. Harry Abrams Inc., 1975.

Funnel, Bertha. *Walt Whitman on Long Island*. Kennikat Press, 1971.

Ganz, Charlotte Adams. *Chronicle of the Head of the River, 1700–1900*.

Handshaw, John E. "Looking Backward or Fragments From a Checkered Life." Published Privately, 1923.

Harris, Bradley. *Black Roots in Smithtown*. Office of Town of Smithtown, July 1986.

Harris, Bradley. "News of Long Ago." *Smithtown News*. 8-30-90; 7-30-81; 11-5-8; 1-21-88; 4-14-88; 10-20-88; 6-8-89; 8-2-90; 9-20-90; 7-30-81; 11-26-81; 2-11-88; 7-7-88; 11-10-88; 6-15-89; 8-9-90; 9-27-90; 8-6-81; 1-5-84; 4-7-88; 7-14-88; 12-1-88; 5-10-90; 8-23-90; 10-10-90.

Harris, Bradley. *The Early History of Kings Park.* Supplement *Smithtown News*, 1983.

Harris, Bradley. *Trees of Smithtown Arbor Day*. Conservation Board, Town of Smithtown, April 26, 1985.

Indian Archaeology of Long Island. Nassau County Museum of Natural History, Leaflet No. 17.

Ketchum, Thomas. A *Business Review of the Nissequogue River from 1830–1900*. Long Island Room, Smithtown Public Library, T.S. 1936.

Langhans, Rufus B. *Place Names in the Town of Smithtown, Their Location, Origin and Meaning*. Smithtown Library, 1961.

Langhart, Nicholas. *Architecture and Town Planning in Smithtown, Long Island, New York, 1665–1825*. Cornell University, 1984.

Latimer, D.M. *Saint Johnland and Its Children.* June 1995.

League of Women Voters. *This is Smithtown*. Smithtown Bicentennial Committee, 1975.

Levine, Gaynell Stone. *Readings in Long Island Archaeology and Ethnohistory*. Suffolk Archaeological Association. Vol. 1–7, 1977–1983.

Long Island Heritage. "The First Purple Heart Earned at Fort Slongo." October 1984.

Luke, Myron and Robert W. Venables. *Long Island in the American Revolution*. New York State Bicentennial Commission, 1976.

Malone, Virginia. *Lending Comforts to the Sick*. Smithtown, 1956.

Marr, Jack. *History of Hauppauge Long Island* (Second Edition), 1981.

_____. "Legacy of Alexander G. Milne." *Long Island Forum*, vol. 49, No. 10, October 1986.

Mehalick, Richard J. *Church and Community 1675–1975 Story of First Presbyterian Church of Smithtown*, 1976.

Mencarelli, Arlene. *Fort Salonga Past and Present*. Fort Salonga Association, 1965.

Mooney, M. Michael. *Evelyn Nesbit and Stanford White*. William Morrow and Co., 1976

Muratore, Nick. Head of River School. File, Smithtown Historical Society.

Murphy, Robert Cushman. *Fish Shaped Paumanauk*. American Philosophical Society, 1964.

Naylor, Natalie. *Exploring African American History*. Long Island Studies Institute, 1991.

Old School Houses. Bicentennial Project. New York State Retired Teachers Association, 1976.

Paddling the Nissequogue Ecological and Historical Guide. Board of Cooperative Educational Services, Suffolk, James Romansky (Editor).

Pelletreau, William Smith. *Records of Town of Smithtown (1715–1835)*. Published by the Town of Smithtown, 1898.

Population Survey 1994. Long Island Lighting Company, July 1994.

Prime Nathaniel S. *A History of Long Island*. Robert S. Carter Co., 1845.

Reynolds, John. *Behind the British Lines During the Revolution*. Society for the Preservation of Long Island Antiquities., 1960.

Rockwell, Verne. *Colonel Rockwell's Scrapbook*. Edited by C.A. Ganz. Smithtown Historical Society, 1968.

Rosen, Lucille. *Commack: A Look into the Past*. Commack Board of Education, 1970.

Ross, Peter. *A History of Long Island*. Vols. 1, 2, 3. Lewis Publishing Co., 1902.

Seyfried, V. F. *The Long Island Railroad*. New York: Garden City, 1961.

Sleight, Harry D. *Records of the Town of Smithtown (1837–1878)*. Published by the Town of Smithtown, 1929.

_____. *Records of the Town of Smithtown (1900–1925)*. Published by the Town of Smithtown, 1930.

Smith, Edward. "Identity of Sarah, wife of Richard Smith of Smithtown, L.I." New York Genealogical and Biographical Record. Vol. 121, no. 1, January 1960.

Smith, Dr. Frederick Kinsman. *The Family of Richard Smith of Smithtown Long Island—Ten Generations*. Smithtown Historical Society, 1967.

Smith, Judge J. Lawrence. *History of Smithtown*. W. W. Munsell Co., 1882.

Smithtown Fire Department Dedication Journal. May 27, 1956.

Smithtown Post Office Dedication Journal. September 27, 1970.

Smithtown Tercentenary Celebration Souvenir Program. Town of Smithtown, August 1936.

Smithtown, Yesterday and Today. Smithtown, 1988.

St. James Methodist Church Journal. Life in St. James, August 19, 1961

____. Our Community, August 19, 1960

____. St. James Methodist Church, August 29, 1964.

Stepanek, Frank A. "Main Street in the Early Days." Antique Automobile, October 1966.

Thompson, Benjamin F. "The History of Long Island." Vol. 1, 2. Gould Bank and Co. First Edition. 1839.

Turrell, Dr. Guy. "The Evolution of a Library." *Long Island Forum*, February/March 1952.

Van Liew, Barbara Ferris. *Fifty Years of Head of the Harbor 1928–1978*. Published by Village of Head of the Harbor, 1978.

Weigold, Marilyn E. *The American Mediterranean: The Long Island Sound*. Kennikat Press, 1974.

Ziel, Ron and George Foster. *Steel Rails to Sunrise*. New York: Hawthorn Books, 1965.

Unpublished Manuscripts

Brush, Frank E. "Early Government," July 1958; "Indians," June 1951; "Mills"; "Nesconset School"; "War of 1812"; "Year of 1816." Notes on File, Smithtown Historical Society.

Dempsey, Tim. Personal Notes on San Remo, 1995.

Harris, Joan Elizabeth. "The Progressive Era in Smithtown, New York: A Study of Five Charitable Institutions." Research Project, Smithtown Historical Society, November 1988.

Hawkins, John. "Botany and History." Smithtown Cemetery Association, 1977.

Irwin, Russell C. "Fort Slongo and it Environs in the Revolutionary War." April 10, 1959.

Onsrud, Laura. "St. Johnland." File, Smithtown Historical Society.

Smith, H.H.R. Letters "From the Civil War, 1861–1865." Smithtown Historical Society File.

Turrell, Virginia. "Bull Smith of Smithtown." Smithtown Historical Society File.

Note on the Brainard Collection: The original 1878 dry plate glass negatives are stored in the Brooklyn Museum. At the time of this publication none of the 2000-piece collection was available for duplication. There are some inter-plate negatives available for viewing at the Brooklyn Public Library, but prints were not available. Some copy prints have found their way to the Queensborough Library, Long Island Collection, and the Society for the Preservation of Long Island Antiquities. S.P.L.I.A. was kind enough to allow reproduction of their collection for this publication.

INDEX

A
A.M.E. Church of Smithtown, 77
Aaron's Landing, 103, 154
Academy, 71
African Americans, 72–81
Allen, Ethan, 49
Andros, Edmund, 23
Arden, Samuel, 77
Arns, William H., 112
Arthur, E. L., 91
Arthur, Erastus, 160
Arthur, Franklin O., 160
Arthur, H. W., 135
Arthur, William, 48, 49, 51
Articles of Association, 45
Asharoken, 143
Automobiles, 108–113

B
Baseball, 131
Beckers Beach, 155
Bertha Friede's Lodge, 152
Bicycles, 107–108
Biggs, Thomas, 150
Bishop, Walter, 86
Blizzard of '88, 144, 163
Blydenburg, William, 154
Blydenburgh Mills, 43
Blydenburgh Park, 41
Blydenburgh's Landing, 30
Blydenburgh, Benjamin, 91
Blydenburgh, Helen, Miss, 172
Blydenburgh, Isaac, 41
Blydenburgh, Joseph, 44, 141
Blydenburgh, Morgan, 80, 175
Blydenburgh, Ruth, widow, 52, 54
Blydenburgh, Vail, 176
Bohemia Club, 124
Bohemia Social Club, 69
Boomertown, 119
Booth and Arthur Store, 91
Booth, George L., 82, 86
Bread and Cheese Hollow, 148
Brooklyn Gun Club, 33, 46
Brooklyn Industrial School Association, 141
Brooklyn Museum, 26
Brown, Lathrop, Mrs., 179
Browning, John Brower, Dr., 104
Brush Barn, 160
Brush, C., Mrs., 180
Brush, Charles, Dr., 176

Brush, Elijah, 68
Brush, Frank, 71, 175
Brush, Mel, 112
Brush, Richard, 184
Bryant, David, 103, 147
Burr family, 145
Burr, Carl S., 89
Burr, Carl S., Jr., 147
Butler Windmill, 124
Butler, Charles S., 99
Butler, Lawrence Smith, 26. 80, 105
Butler, Prescott H., Mrs., 80

C
Caleb Smith Park, 40
Call, William, 164
Carman Farm, 122
Census of 1776, 15
Central Hotel, 164
Churchill, Elijah, 148
Clayton, William H., 99
Clinton, George, Governor, 65
Clinton, Henry, Sir, 53
Collier, Willie, 124
Commack Corners, 143, 145
Commack North, 66
Commack South, 68
Commack, 100, 143–147
Commack (schooner), 174
Common crossing, 34
Conklin, Harold, 176
Cook, Philander, 83, 84
Cornwallis, General, 51, 53
Courriere Holding Company, 156
Cusick, George, 133, 176
Cusick, John J., 108

D
Darling, Adam, 154
Darling, C. B., 97
Darling, Hamilton, 154
Darling, John, 55, 56
Darling, W. F., Mrs., 172
Debating Society, 57
Deepwells, 117
Denton, Daniel, 59
Deutzman, Lawrence F., 179, 183
Dewing, Oliver M., Dr., 129
Dobbs, Charles, 77
Dowling, Cornelius, 176
Ducey, Reverend Father, 183

E
Eagle Hook and Ladder Company, 100
East Riding, 23
Ebenezer Smith General Store, 118
Education, 65–73
Edwards, Mae, 94
Edwards, Paul, Mrs., 180
Edwards, William, Reverend, 80
Emancipation Proclamation, 79
Epenetus Smith Tavern, 160
Evans, J., 108
Everett Hand, 71

F
Fanning, George T., 107
Fire Department, 95–101
Firehouse, 100
First World War, 175–177
Fitzpatrick, N. P., 85
Floyd, William, 45, 47
Ford Motor Agency, 112
Fort Salonga (Slongo), 51, 148–149
Fresh Pond, 148
Friede, Bertha, 153
Friede, Frank, 32

G
Gallaghers Avenue, 121
Gardiner, Lion, 20
Garnet, Hervey Highland, Reverend, D.D., 77, 79
Gaynor, William, Mayor, 117, 152, 153
George Thompson's Store, 132
Golden Hill, 164
Gould, Blanche E., 180
Greek Orthodox Church, 156

H
Halliock (Hallock), Thomas, 55
Halliock, Thomas, 167
Hallock Blacksmith Shop, 93, 97, 163
Hallock Inn, 68, 85, 167
Hallock, 160
Hallock, George, 176
Hallock, William Meritt, 151
Hammond, Sarah, 24
Handley's dock, 156
Handley, Richard H., 107, 108, 137, 155, 156, 169
Handley, Richard, Mrs., 80
Harned, Burtis S., 144

Harriman, W. Averill, 26
Hart, Joshua, 49
Hauppauge Methodist Church, 139
Hauppauge Village Hall, 140
Hauppauge, 56, 137–142
Hauppauge (schooner), 174
Hawkins, Frank, Captain, 32
Head of the Harbor, 119
Head of the River School, 65
Head of the River, 34, 61, 91
Head of the River, 159
Higgins, Charles M., 39
Hilander, Dr., 134
Howard Colored Orphan Asylum, 79
Howell, William, 113
Hoyt Farm, 146
Hoyt, Edwin Chase, 146
Hubbs, Kenneth, 112
Hunting House, 160
Hunting, J. S., 97

I
Indian Head Road, 17, 132

J
J. S. Huntting Store, 92, 161
Jackson, Ethalinda, 169
Jarrett, Isaac, 61
Jaynes, W. Benjamin, 91
Jim Ferraro's Grocery, 157
John of London (ship), 19
Jones, Rosalie, 179
Joshua Smith house, 140

K
Kenyon family, 39
Ketcham Brothers, 35
Kidd's Money Hole, 148
Kings Park Hook and Ladder Company, 99
Kings Park Hospital Fire Department, 101
Kings Park schoolroom, 70
Kohr, Gus, 132
Ku Klux Klan, 181–183
Kutil, Mr., 153
Kutil, Mrs., 153

L
L'Hommedieu, Guy, 176
Lady Suffolk, 103, 105, 147
Lake Avenue, 121

Lake Ronkonkoma Equal Rights Suffrage Club, 179
Lake Ronkonkoma Ice Boat and Yacht Club, 150
Lake Ronkonkoma, 16, 150–151
Landing Avenue Bridge, 30
Landing Avenue, 36
Lange, Edward, 102, 126
Lawrence, Arthur B., 104
Lawrence, Charles E., Mrs., 80
Lawrence, Leonard W., 103, 154
Lawrence, R., Mr., 105
Library association, 166
Lincoln, Abraham, 83
Lindbergh, Charles, 184–185
Little Beach, 63
Locustdale Home for Children, 142
Locustdale, 79, 141
Long Beach, 63
Long Island Auto Club, 110
Long Island Motor Parkway, 110, 146
Long Island Railroad, 36, 88–90, 107

M
Macy, Dr., 131
Maple Avenue, 162
Massachusetts Bay Colony, 19
Matinecock, 22
Methodist Parsonage, 160
Miller, Charles A., Mrs., 80
Miller, Charles D., 164
Miller, H. W., 135
Miller, James Ely, 177
Mills Family, 37
Mills Pond House, 116
Mills, Martha, 180
Mills, Mary Emma (Minnie), 80
Mills, Timothy, 116
Moffat, Gertrude, Miss, 173
Monahan's Blacksmith and Wheelwright Shop, 119, 121
Monahan, W. H., 119
Mount, Shepard A., 74
Mount, William S., 74
Muhlenberg, William Augustus, 127
Munro, Donald C., 177

N
NAACP, 80
Nasseconseke (Nesconset), 17
Native Americans, 16–18

Nellie A. Ryle (sloop), 32
Nesconset, 22
Nesconset (ship), 153
Nesequake, 16
New Mill Pond, 61
New Mill, 42
Newton, William E., 68
Nichols Family, 166
Nicolls Patent, 22
Nicolls, Frank, 176
Nicolls, Richard, 22
Nicosia, Charles, 153
Nissequogue Canning Company, 37
Nissequogue Hotel, 121
Nissequogue Trout Club, 39
Nissequogue River, 31–40, 159
Nissequogue (village), 119

O
O'Berry, John, Mr., 99
O'Berry, Norman, 178
Okst, Jacob, 134
Old Library, 160
Old Mill, 41
Olivie, Bernard, 39

P
Pardington, Arthur Raynor, 109, 111
Patiky, Elias, 129, 131, 134, 134, 135
Patiky, Gershon, 131, 131, 134
Patiky, Jennie, 134
Patiky, Ruth, 131
Paumanauk, 16
Payne, Wessels, 87
Pedrick, Hattie, 169
Peek, Cornelia, 80, 169, 180
Peterson, Frederick, Dr., 172
Peterson, Frederick, Mrs., 175, 179
Phillips' Mills, 41, 61
Phillips, George, 41, 91
Phillips, Mills, 154
Pig Creek, 63
Plague of 1658–59, 18
Platt, Nathaniel, 45
Platt, Zephaniah, 47
Post Office, 91
Potatoes, 59
Presbyterian Church, 40, 48
Presbyterian Manse, 160
Prescott Hall Butler windmill, 123
Prime, Nathaniel, 77

Progresso, Il, 156
Prohibition, 180

R
Radoyevich, Boris, 39
Rassapeaque Club, 38
Reading Room, 167
Reisert, William, 135
Revolution, 45–53
Ritch, Wilson, Jr., 175
River Road, 114
Riverside Garage, 110
Riverside Hotel, 32
Riverside Inn, 35
Rockwell, Charles Embree, 184
Roosevelt, Theodore, 113
Royal Arcanum Hall, 92
Rumsey, Charles Cary, 26

S
Saints Philip and James Catholic Church, 125
San Remo, 154, 157–158
Sanford, Charles, 162
Schecter, Mr., 183
Seaman, Elias, 39
Seaman, Mary H., 180
Setauket, 20
Sheep, 61
Sherreowogue, 123
Ships hole, 35
Shore Inn, The, 120
Short Beach, 32
Skidmore,
   Nathaniel, 51
Slavery, 72
Smith I, Caleb, 47
Smith II, Caleb, 41, 139, 143
Smith II, Daniel, 137
Smith II, Epenetus, 65
Smith, Aaron, 89, 154
Smith, Abner, 51
Smith, Adam, 41, 115, 117, 123
Smith, Caleb Tangier, 115
Smith, Caleb, 41, 54
Smith, Joshua II, 41
Smith, Caleb, 61
Smith, Coe D., 108
Smith, Daniel A., 68
Smith, Daniel, 148
Smith, Dorothy Miller, 179
Smith, E. Captain, 150

Smith, E. H., 84
Smith, E. T., 135
Smith, Ebenezer, 61, 115
Smith, Ebenezer, Major, 139, 141
Smith, Edmund, 176
Smith, Edmund, Jr., 45, 75
Smith, Edward H. L., 112
Smith, Edward H. L., Mrs., 80
Smith, Edward Henry, 85
Smith, Elias, 154
Smith, Epenetus, 77
Smith, Harry, 112, 176
Smith, Henry Chatfield, Mrs., 172
Smith, James Clinch, 105
Smith, Job, 115
Smith, Joel L. G., 85, 89
Smith, Jonas, 68
Smith, Jonathan, 115
Smith, Joseph, 116
Smith, Josephine, 104
Smith, Joshua, 139, 141
Smith, Joshua II, 41
Smith, Lawrence, 176
Smith, Lawrence, Judge, 68, 85, 168
Smith, Lyman Beecher, 68
Smith, Nancy, 51
Smith, Obadiah, 25
Smith, Paul Theodore, 41
Smith, Phebe Tredwell, 154
Smith, Philetus, 154
Smith, Richard, 15, 17, 19–25, 59, 61, 72,
   115, 137, 143, 148
Smith, Robert, 176
Smith, Samuel Arden, 79
Smith, Samuel, 45, 115
Smith, Sarah, 148
Smith, Solomon, 96
Smith, Theodore W., Mrs., 80
Smith, Timothy, 116
Smith, W. Ward, 135
Smith, William E., 94
Smithtown Automobile Company, 109
Smithtown Branch High School Baseball Team
   of 1928, 73
Smithtown Branch High School, 73
Smithtown Branch Post Office, 92
Smithtown Debating Society, 57
Smithtown Girls' Basketball Team of 1924–25,
   73
Smithtown Hunt, 105
Smithtown Messenger, 179

Smithtown Messenger, 183
Smithtown Methodist Church, 162
Smithtown Polo Club, 105
Smithtown Post Office, 91
Smithtown Railroad Station, 94
Smithtown Volunteer Hook and Ladder Company, 97
Smithtown-Port Jefferson Railroad, 88
Society for Lending Comforts to the Sick, 172
Society of St. Johnland, 129
Soper, Strong, 86
Southampton, 20
Spahr, Ada F., 180
Spahr, Henry, 161
Spahr, William, 161
Spofera, Nicolas, 153
Spofera, Paul, 153
Spurge, William, 32
St. James Elementary School, 69
St. James Fire Department, 99
St. James General Store, 118
St. James Hotel, 120
St. James Lutheran Church, 125
St. James Methodist Church, 125
St. James, 115
St. Johnland, 79, 97, 126, 127
St. Joseph's Catholic Church, 134
St. Patrick's Church, 138, 139
Stony Brook Harbor, 121
Stump Pond, 41
Sturm, Charles, 163
Suffragettes, 179
Sunken Meadow Creek, 47

T
Tanner (brig), 32
Tarleton, Banastre, Colonel, 49
Telephone, 93–95
Temple Beth Chai, 140
Thompson, George L., State Senator, 135, 179
Three Sisters Harbor, 117
Titanic (ship), 105
Town Hall, 159, 166
Trainors Hotel, 99
Treadwells Neck, 51, 148
Tredwell, Thomas, 53, 75
Turner, Arthur, 151
Turrell, Guy H., Dr., 172
Tyler, Edward H., Mrs., 172
Tyler, Emma A., 180

U
Upjohn, Richard, 119

V
Vail, John, 55
Valentine, Antoinette, 153
Valentine, Frank, 112, 113, 153
Valentine, Jimmy, 153
Valentine, Louis, 153
Valentine, Nick, 153
Van Brunt, Minnie, 169
Vanderbilt, William Kissam, 109
Village of the Branch, 159
Vion family, 153
Vion, Louis, 153

W
W.C.T.U., 180
Wallabout Bay, 47
Walsh's Saloon, 132
Washington, George, 54
Webster Pond, 38
Webster, Daniel, 37
Weismann, Henry, 99
Wetherell, 123
Wheeler, Jacob, 49
Wheeler, Mary Jane, 56
Wheeler, Thomas, 137
Whisper (bull), 24, 26
Whitaker, Henry B., 153
White, Stanford, 122
Whitman School House, 65
Whitman, Walt, 57, 66, 68, 145
Wicks Farm, 146
Wicks, Elnathan, 147
Wicks, John, 147
Williams, Buell, Mrs., 172
Willow Pond, 41
Wood, John, Mrs., 95
Woodhull, William, 55
Wright, Joseph, 46
Wyandanch Club, 33, 46
Wyandanch, 20, 22, 143

Y
York Lots, 49

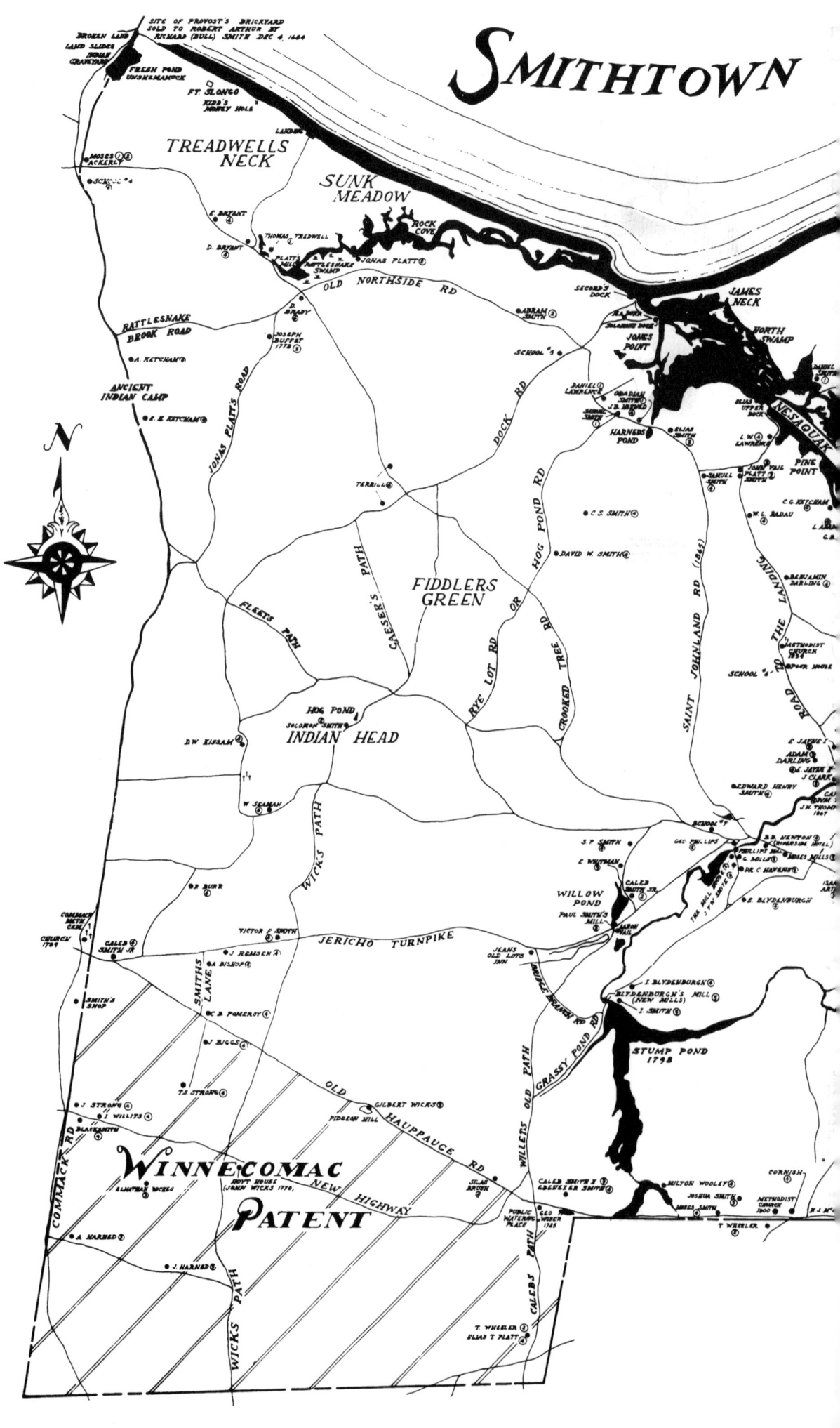